Debut A New You

Transforming Your Life At Any Age

Publishing and Design:

Quantity sales. Special discounts are available on quantity purchases by corporations, associations, and others. For details, contact the publisher at the address above. Orders by U.S. trade book-stores and wholesalers.

Contact: 800-273-1625 | support@epicauthor.com | EpicAuthor.com

For more information about Dr. Mimi Secor or to book her for your next event or media interview, visit: MimiSecor.com

Debut A New You

Transforming Your Life At Any Age

HEALTH.
CONFIDENCE.
SUCCESS.

Dr. Mimi Secor

Book Bonuses

"Please get the fantastic bonuses my daughter and I created to help you jumpstart your success. I think you're going to love it!"
-Dr. Mimi

To get the 24 hour Solution go to:
www.DebutANewYou.com

Table of Contents

Dedication

To all the patients, nurse practitioners, and people I meet
in my travels who have inspired me to write this book
and walk my talk.

Foreword

THIS BOOK WAS CONCEIVED as a celebration of living a full life, and as a testament that you can achieve the lifestyle and body you desire at any age. Often as we get older, the expectation of high achievement and big dreams of our youth diminishes with each passing year. People often stop trying new things, stop creating, and may even stop using their imaginations. Our call to "live life to the fullest" somehow seems to no longer apply in the second half of our lives.

My mother, Mimi is a role model, showing that the best days of your life can be the ones you are living right now—in this moment, at any age. Even if you're 60, 70, or 80, nothing is too far from your grasp. Living life to the fullest, dreaming big dreams, and achieving those dreams is possible at any age. The only thing that holds us back is our belief in our own abilities and limitations. My mom often says, "We must believe to achieve."

I look up to my mother for so many reasons, but the most important of which is that she's human. She's vulnerable. She is not invincible, nor is she any different from you or me. In fact, the only difference between her and the majority of people who still struggle is that she actively practices getting out of her comfort zone, and has dedicated her life to doing whatever it takes to achieve her goals. These are the principles she outlines in this book.

Living life to the fullest means trying new things, and not allowing the fear of failure to hold you back from loving yourself or your life. My mother is proof that at any age we can dream big, and pursue those dreams until they become our reality. I hope that my mother's journey will be an inspiration to both women and men, wherever they are in their lives regardless of their age.

—Katherine "Kat" Secor, IFBB (International Federation of Bodybuilding) and Fitness Pro

Introduction

AT 62 YEARS OF AGE, I never thought I would be buying a bikini for myself. The store assistant who was about my age thought I was buying it for my daughter! When she realized it was for me, she said, "Must be great to wear one of those!"

Yes, it's great! But it's not just the physical image that matters. It was the fact that only a few years ago, I never dreamed that it would be possible to look really great but also to feel so good about my life.

At the time, I was speaking nationally as a nurse practitioner, traveling around the country attending lots of conferences. Through the eyes of outside observers, I was living the dream life.

On top of that, I was also working on my doctorate, racing against time to meet my assignment deadlines!

But it was all overwhelming. I wasn't sleeping well. I wasn't eating well. I had no time to exercise, (or so I thought!) and I was stressed out. No surprise, I was gaining weight (what felt like by the minute) and was on track to being 50 pounds overweight by the time of my graduation.

During that time, I *knew* something had to change. I knew what I needed to do, but I always found an excuse *not to* do it ...

- "I don't have time for this!"

- "It's too expensive to hire a trainer."

- "I'm too old for this."

- "I've tried dieting and exercise; it doesn't work!"

- "I'm too stressed to even think about getting healthy."

- "I have no idea where to start."

- "My life is too complicated."

- "I know what I should do but..." "I'm not a morning person." "...It's too late in the day to exercise."

The truth is, my weight has been up and down like a yo-yo all my life. Even though I lived an active lifestyle most of my life: cycling, walking, skiing—my weight fluctuated.

By age 59, I had mostly given up on the hope for things to be any different.

Thankfully, I got a wake-up call from my daughter:

> *"Mom, you can't keep going in this direction. You cannot let the wheels fall off your wagon like this. You're going to crash-and-burn. At this rate, you will be 50 pounds overweight when you graduate; is that what you want?"*

I responded:

> *"No, I don't want to crash-and-burn. I really don't! But honest to God, I don't think there's anything anyone can do to help me."*

I truly didn't believe anyone could help me.

But Kat inspired me to take a step back to look at my situation.

She's a natural-born coach in that respect, which is what led to her nickname, Coach Kat.

As an IFBB Pro Bodybuilder in the Women's Physique division and an ISSA (International Sports Sciences Association) certified fitness trainer, Kat is passionate about helping women and men make lifelong health and lifestyle transformations. I am very proud of her and thrilled to now be working with her in our shared health/fitness/transformation business.

That day, she became instrumental in helping *me* transform *my life*.

With Kat's help, I realized the hypocrisy of my situation. I started wondering what message was I sending to my patients when I couldn't even manage my own stress and well-being?

3

I wasn't walking my talk. And I certainly wasn't being a role model to my patients, family or community.

Determined, and with Coach Kat's help, I started eating clean and took up weightlifting to rebuild my body, deal with stress, and to take control of my life again. But this time, I decided, I wasn't going to do it alone. So, in addition to working with my daughter I also hired a trainer.

That's when I realized *why* I'd never lost weight in the past, and kept it off. I would lose weight, only to gain it back (plus some) and be in worse shape than when I started. One step forward, two-steps backward.

Maybe you're so busy you can't even take time to go to the bathroom, eat a meal, let alone...work out!

Maybe you feel obligated to put other people's needs first, so your own needs get neglected.

Perhaps you tell yourself, *I've tried EVERYTHING, and nothing is EVER going to work out for me*!

Maybe you've tried all the diets available on the market.

And no matter how hard you try, you either struggle to have more energy, keep your weight off, or to feel good in your own skin.

I know *exactly* what you mean. But guess what? You are not alone. There is a way to turn things around, and in this book, I will show you how.

I thought I was eating a healthy diet for years. I didn't understand why I kept gaining weight back after losing it. I did not appreciate aspects of nutrition that are truly make or break concepts. For instance, I learned about the significance of "invisible calories," recording our food (all of it), and the fact that every calorie counts but that every calorie is not created equal. I learned about portion control and hidden calories in "healthy" foods, etc.

First, you must realize that exercise and nutrition are just <u>one part</u> of the equation. You need to integrate all aspects of your mind, body, and spirit, to achieve a lasting full-life transformation.

Second, the solution to your situation lies in a domain you don't even know exists. It's like trying to look behind your eyes. That's why you need a team. That's why you need a coach. So, let me be that coach for you.

Together, we will explore how to optimize your nutrition, exercise, mindset, environment, and team.

Using my newfound knowledge and skills, I made my bodybuilding "Debut at 62" winning fifth place in the novice over 40 category (most contestants were 20 years younger); I regained my energy, and more importantly, my confidence to pursue and create my dream life.

You'll find out more about my journey in the coming chapters.

Here's what I learned:

- It's never too late (and you are never too old) to make a big change to transform your health and your life.

- It's never too late to pursue your dreams or take on a new challenge. Heck, I was 59 when I decided to go back to school and earn my doctorate!

And.... _Age is just a number._

Today, I enjoy spending lots of time with my amazing daughter Kat, and together, we own and operate our coaching business (**www.CoachKatandDoctorMimi.com**), empowering nurse practitioners, healthcare professionals and busy on-the-go women and men with the tools and know-how to transform their health and their lives.

What you will learn in this book isn't just about weightlifting and cardio. It isn't just about bodybuilding and getting the body of your dreams. You don't have to enter a competition to learn the principles that will transform your life.

What you will learn in this book can be used to empower _any aspects_ of your life: relationships, personal purpose, career, health, physical appearance, etc.

- Gain the personal confidence and power to overcome any challenge in life.

- Look and feel good in your own skin (even naked!)

- Have more energy.

- Get more done with less effort.

- Gain the conviction to be who you want to be, so you can offer the world your authentic and awesome self.

- Reduce your stress levels.

- Deepen relationships with family, friends, and loved ones.

- Open new opportunities in your career, business, and life.

I'm so excited about sharing with you, my health and fitness journey. It is my hope that I will inspire and guide you in transforming your life so you can "Debut a New You," too and live your dream life. I want you to be healthier, more confident and successful as much as you want it for yourself.

In the first chapter, I will discuss why it is so important to make a 100 percent commitment to your health goals and your personal transformation.

In the next four sections, I will cover vital aspects of nutrition, exercise, mindset, and environment that must be addressed to successfully transform your life and achieve your goals and dreams!

Being fully committed to your goals and your transformaion is essential to achieving your dreams. If you are not all in, then when your journey becomes challenging, and it will, you will be at risk of throwing in the towel and grabbing your favorite goodies. Guaranteed.

You must dig deep into your soul/thoughts/self-beliefs and consider these areas of your life before you waste time on yet another attempt at changing your circumstances. This is precisely why I address mindset in my book. I am passionate about helping you transform your life now and over time. Sustained change is only possible if you have cleaned your inner house AKA your mind.

Both my personal experience and my experience in working with patients for over 40 years as a nurse practitioner reinforces the importance of this concept.

With each passing day that I commit to walking my talk as a healthy role model for others, I realize that our successes and failures are very closely linked to our self-commitment, (and self-image—what we think of ourselves), self-awareness and personal insight into what makes us tick.

When we address and adjust these key elements of our mindset, we can truly make lasting change.

Join me as we embark on this exciting journey together, and I will share with you step-by-step what you need to know (and do) to totally transform your life (at any age.)

Are you ready to *Debut a New You,* and start transforming your life? Let's get started...

Dr. Mimi

Section I:
COMMITMENT

CHAPTER 1

5 Principles To Jump Start Your Health

D ID YOU KNOW THAT a staggering 92 percent of people who set New Year's goals never achieve them?

Case in point: one study examined the success rate of 200 people who had set New Year's resolutions. They tracked the resolvers over two years in an effort to identify the determining factors of what caused people to succeed in their resolutions. According to the study, "Successful resolvers reported employing significantly more stimulus control, reinforcement, and willpower than the unsuccessful over the two years; social support and interpersonal strategies failed to predict success before six months but did so thereafter. Counterconditioning and fading, developing new skills and habits and phasing out unhealthy habits were retrospectively nominated as the most efficacious coping strategies; paucity of willpower and failure of stimulus control were reported as the most hindering to maintenance. Fifty-three percent of the successful group experienced at least one slip, and the mean number of slips over the two-year interval was fourteen. Slips were typically precipitated by a lack of personal control, excessive stress, and negative emotion."

This is why a positive attitude, expert self-care, and coping skills are so essential to our success in achieving both our short and long-term health goals.

If you want to achieve your resolutions, setting specific and challenging goals is one approach you can apply to your intentions. Those who are not clear on what their goals will be and how they will go about reaching them are more likely to fail. The theory is that the more specific you can get in defining your goals and the harder you make them, the higher your motivation will be.

If you were to set a goal of wanting to lose 20 pounds by the end of the year (a goal many, many people make on a daily basis), you might be surprised to find out that this aim is actually a little vague.

You want to get specific with the actions you will take and how you plan on tackling your obstacles. You might do this by stating: "In August, I will lose five pounds when I cut out refined sugar, breads, and fast food. I will walk at a rapid pace for 20 minutes every day as well."

It's amazing when you become super clear, how much more likely you are to reach your goals. Break down your overwhelming goals into bite-sized chunks, or doable tasks. What's the saying? *Eat the elephant one bite at a time.* You can apply the same thought process and take smaller steps that will lead to your bigger goals as you navigate your new course to success.

Huffington Post's article, "10 Reasons We Fail to Achieve Our Goals," notes the following main reasons people do not meet their objectives.

1. Excuses.

2. Magnifying our fears more than our abilities, fear of failure.

3. Not having a strong enough why.

4. Not setting the right priorities.

5. Trying your hand at everything. (That used to be me).

6. Crying wolf too often. Telling people, you want to do something too many times and not doing it.

7. Lacking a plan.

8. Not being committed.

9. Or, not having a deadline.

10. Giving up when the going gets tough.

So, remember, when you are tackling your goals, break them down into tangible, simple and super attainable chunks. Number one, keep it simple. Number two, make it tangible.

You have as much willpower as you think you have. Contrary to what you may think, we have control over our destiny. Consider this.

Are you ready? Bring an open mind, plus your 100 percent commitment and let's jump in!

Speaking of jumping in, Katherine has an amazing way of simplifying this jump-start process. The first five lessons she taught me, I now affectionately refer to as Coach Kat's 5 Principles to Jump Start Your Health Journey. These have not only helped *me* to think differently and transform my life but have helped numerous other women and men who she's worked with over the years.

Contrary to popular belief, the journey to healthy living doesn't have to be complicated. By demystifying the process, we've already positioned ourselves onto the road of success. You can get started by implementing these five principles into your own life.

Here are the 5 Principles:

- Principle #1: Take Responsibility for Your Health

- Principle #2: Stop Guessing

- Principle #3: Food Is Fuel

- Principle #4: Exercise Is Enjoyable

- Principle #5: Commit 100 Percent

Principle #1: Take Responsibility For Your Health

You and you alone are responsible for the food you put into your body. What you eat should be based on the amount of exercise you're getting on a daily basis, the lifestyle you want to lead, and the type of physique you desire to have.

What are your standards for yourself? I challenge you to raise the bar. I also challenge you to take charge of your life, and not become a casualty of unconscious ignorance. I often say, "Inevitable decline of aging is not inevitable."

Principle #2: Stop Guessing

You don't have to count every calorie. But to achieve any goal, you *must* have a plan and take measurable action. By knowing what you're eating, and how much you're eating, you are more likely to achieve your short *and* long-term weight loss goals.

Principle #3: Food Is Fuel

Our bodies need nutrients and fluids to function optimally. The nutrients we consume are the fuel our bodies use to energize us, to change, grow and heal. Instead of using the food as a reward, think about using it as fuel for your body to improve health.

Principle #4: Exercise Is Enjoyable

Incorporate exercise that is *fun* into your weekly regimen. If you're doing something you enjoy, you have a far greater chance of continuing it and remaining consistent. It's this consistency that will help you achieve your goals over a longer period of time. Do you prefer swimming, walking, running, cycling, kickboxing, martial arts, yoga, or maybe group exercise classes?

Principle #5: Commit 100 Percent

As John Assaraf says, "If you're interested, you will do what is convenient. If you're committed, you will do whatever it takes." So, let me ask you, are you interested, or are you fully committed?

Section II:
NUTRITION

CHAPTER 2

An "Easy" Eating Plan

ACCORDING TO THE CENTERS for Disease Control and Prevention (CDC), more than one-third of adults in the United States are obese. Obesity-related conditions include stroke, Type 2 Diabetes, heart disease, and certain types of cancer. Non-Hispanic blacks have the highest rates of obesity at 48.1 percent followed by Hispanics at 42.5 percent and non-Hispanic whites at 34.5 percent. Women earning a higher income are less likely to be diagnosed as obese than lower income women. The most recent estimates of annual medical costs for obesity in the United States were $147 billion. Medical costs for people who are obese were $1,429 higher than those of normal weight. Obesity now affects one in six children and adolescents in the United States. Obesity is increasingly common, serious, and very costly. *If you think making a change is expensive, think about the cost of not making a change.*

You will be happy to know that creating and following a healthy eating plan is essential for good health and not that hard to figure out. The best eating plan is one you like and that you will follow over time. That is what we will cover in this chapter.

Diet Is "Die With A T"

I believe "diet" is a negative word and joke that it symbolizes "die with a T." If you think about it, the word implies deprivation and that you will reach an endpoint. A healthy eating plan should not feel like punishment or as if you are depriving yourself. An appropriate and optimal eating plan should be appealing and long-term. To figure out the right one for you, you can ask Coach Kat as well as follow a basic healthy eating plan that includes all food groups.

This should include 1. Moderate amounts of lean protein (at least three times a day), 2. Generous amounts of low glycemic vegetables (5-11 servings a day) (green veggies will give you the best benefits) and small amounts of higher glycemic vegetables (corn, peas, lima beans) and fruits. Fruits are so healthy and good for us, but they are also fairly high in calories, so you want to be aware of the amount you consume. 3. Small to moderate amounts of complex, unprocessed carbohydrates (brown rice, sweet potatoes, whole wheat pasta, or bread). A typical serving size of carbs (2-3 servings a day) is approximately one-half cup which is about the size of a lime or very large egg. This quantity is not a large serving platter. Think about the last time you went out for Italian food and the quantity of pasta they served you. Usually, it's much more than you should consume in a single serving. 4. Small amounts of good healthy fats (olive oil, avocado, and nuts.) These are calorie dense, and add up quickly. That's why you want to keep your intake on the lower side. 5. Adequate water is also essential.

It's also critically important especially if you are seeking to lose weight that you appreciate quantities and calories of these foods and food groups.

A serving of protein is about four ounces, and that's approximately the size of a deck of cards. How easy is that to remember? If you're eating fish, you will use a double deck of cards because fish is very low-calorie. However, here's a warning. Fish is low-calorie *if* it is poached, grilled or broiled-without basting or finish sauce. But, if it is *deep-fried, stuffed or in a sauce* then it can be very high in calories. So, beware when eating out!

This is true for vegetables as well. Often, at restaurants or when we're visiting friends, butter and sauces are added to the vegetables, and then you really have no idea of the calorie count. If the veggies appear shiny then probably oil or butter was added.

25

This is true for salads as well. In fact, salads are deceptive. Salads are potentially healthy however they frequently contain very high-calorie items such as nuts, dried fruits, yummy delicious cheeses, and croutons. You name it, and it may be on your salad. It's best if you get into the habit of asking for a salad but request that they hold all those high-calorie items. You can also ask for them (and the dressing) on the side. I don't even use salad dressing anymore. I like plain salads. I don't want to waste my calories on salad dressing plus I find it masks the flavor of the salad ingredients. But, it was a long process, literally of years of practicing this food habit to get to the point where I prefer salad without dressing. As you go through this process, cut yourself some slack and give yourself time to make adjustments. I used to love bleu cheese crumbles and bleu cheese dressing and now finally, I can enjoy a salad without bleu cheese of any kind, and that's a victory.

Finally, your healthy eating plan generally should include at least three meals a day starting with a healthy protein-packed breakfast. Cold or even hot cereal is not usually high in protein. You can add protein to hot cereal (or cold cereal for that matter), but typically, people do not get as much protein with either of these breakfast foods as compared to eating eggs or Greek yogurt—perhaps with nuts or other protein alternatives. Taking time to eat a lunch even if it's a quick lunch will help keep you going throughout the afternoon. Your goal should also be to have a dinner that's not too large but is healthy. This is a great way to end your day.

Skipping meals throughout the day is problematic for many reasons. First, skipping meals slows down your metabolism, so you will not burn as many calories. You may ironically gain weight from this habit. For most people, there are few advantages to skipping meals.

Another problem with skipping meals is that you are more likely to crave unhealthy foods throughout the day because you're hungry. One of the major advantages of eating regular healthy meals throughout the day is that it suppresses your hunger. Water helps suppress hunger also. In fact, did you know sometimes when you feel hungry, you may actually be thirsty?

Eating regular meals also helps mental concentration, which allows you to make better decisions and helps you to stabilize your moods.

The worst thing you can do is go all day without eating and then arrive home starving and pig out on a huge meal, lots of junk food, not to mention the possibility of perhaps consuming too much alcohol.

Here are a few more startling statistics to consider.

80 percent of weight loss is diet-related.

60 percent of people are overweight.

30 percent are obese.

The National Weight Control Registry (NWCR) was developed to identify and investigate the characteristics of individuals who have succeeded at long-term weight loss. They are tracking over 5,000 individuals who have lost significant amounts of weight and kept it off for long periods of time.

If you want further information from reputable sites, here are a few more resources.

ChooseMyPlate.gov

USDA's Choose MyPlate website features practical information and tips to help Americans build healthier diets. Their Daily Food Plan shows what and how much to eat based on your calorie allowance. Your food plan is personalized by age, gender, height, weight, and physical activity level.

Health.gov/dietaryguidelines

Containing dietary guidelines for Americans, and published jointly by the Department of Health and Human Services (HHS) and the Department of Agriculture (USDA), this site provides advice about how good dietary habits for people aged two years and older can promote health and reduce the risk for major chronic diseases.

Heart.org/HEARTORG/HealthyLiving/ FatsAndOils/Fats101

This is the valuable and reliable **Face the Fat, AHA Fat Calculator.** The American Heart Association's (AHA) tool helps to take the guesswork out of eating fat and encourages smarter fat choices.

Portion Distortion

Do you know how food portions have changed in 20 years? Take this quiz from the National Institutes of Health (NIH.)

The Usda, Food And Nutrition Information Center's (Fnic) Interactive Tools

These websites help consumers and professionals through an array of interactive tools for dietary assessment and planning, checking personal health risks, testing knowledge, and evaluating needs.

Centers For Disease Control And Prevention

www.cdc.gov/healthyweight/tools/index.html

Offers meal planning and tracking tools for 2017.

SuperTracker

USDA's Choose MyPlate SuperTracker can help you plan, analyze, and track your diet and physical activity. Find out what and how much to eat; track foods, physical activities, and weight; and personalize using goal setting, virtual coaching, and journaling.

TWO UNCONVENTIONAL BUT TOTALLY SUCCESSFUL STRATEGIES

1. "Treat" Meal Vs. "Cheat" Meal

Believe it or not, while I was getting ready for my competition, this is what my show coach told me to do.

"Mimi, it's important that you cheat once in a while. Once a week, you should have a cheeseburger with a few fries, or a little bit of dessert."

In the bodybuilding world, this is referred to as a "Cheat Meal," but I prefer to refer to it as a "Treat Meal." I will explain the difference in verbiage shortly. It was my show coach's suggestion that I indulge in a weekly "Treat Meal."

Contrary to popular belief, you shouldn't just stick to a basic routine all the time. That's because our bodies get used to whatever the basic routine is, and as a result, our metabolism can slow down. I call this metabolic complacency.

I didn't start introducing a treat meal into my plan until I started working with my show coach in the spring of 2016. I was stalled out when I first met with him in terms of plateauing with my weight. A treat meal, even during show prep can be helpful to boost metabolism.

The occasional treat meal can jump start us, just as we would jump start a car with a dead battery. It can rev up our metabolism, and in fact, help us burn more calories throughout the following week. This is not an extreme situation of caloric surplus; it's a modest amount. I've been able to maintain my weight—if not lose a little—while allowing myself an occasional treat. I love it, but I get anxious about the prospect at the same time. This is because when you increase carbohydrates, you also increase fluid retention. This means your weight will naturally bump up for a few days. Even though I still panic when my weight bumps up after my treat meal, I know it will go back down and that the concept works. It has worked for me for almost a year now!

To boost your metabolism and address cravings, consider having a "treat meal" once a week, maybe on Saturday nights. I've come to appreciate I can enjoy treats now and again, as long as they're in the context of a calculated eating program. Your favorite foods don't have to be forbidden forever. When you realize that, it is a liberating perspective.

The difference between a "Cheat Meal" and a "Treat Meal" is huge. Cheat implies that somehow we are misbehaving. Treat implies a reward. And that's exactly what a treat meal is—a higher calorie meal (usually including carbohydrates and fats) that is eaten to boost metabolism. This combats what happens when our caloric intake is the same over a period of time (weeks and/or months). This is because our bodies are very efficient and adjust quickly to a steady calorie intake by slowing down to conserve energy. It is thought that this physiologic phenomenon dates back to our caveman ancestry when we had no idea where our next meal would come from. So, conserving energy was life-saving. That is not the case in the modern world. In fact, food is omnipresent for most populations in industrialized countries.

I cannot overstate how much I look forward to my once a week treat meal. The idea of it keeps me going during the week. So, when I feel like throwing in the towel and giving up on my show prep eating plan, I think about my treat meal. I also tell myself that going off my eating plan will not help me reach my goal. Then I remind myself how much I want to reach my goal. So, instead of focusing on the here and now and wanting a treat, I think about what I would like to indulge in, on Saturday night when I have my treat meal. This fantasy sustains me through most weeks, and that's priceless.

2. Portion Control And Awareness

Frequently, I get asked, "What do you eat?" "When do you eat it?" "What's your magic nutritional formula?" Although everyone's nutritional needs are different, I've found for me it's best to eat 20 grams (four ounces) of protein every three hours to create a nice, steady blood sugar level. My body needs this, even though it's higher than the American Dietetic Association (ADA) recommendation of 45-56 grams of protein for adults with average activity, depending on gender and body weight. While researching this subject, I realized I was making the transition from average-active-person into more of an athlete category. For endurance and strength-trained athletes, this changes the recommended protein intake from the ADA to 90-114 grams per day. It was an interesting revelation for me, especially at 62 years of age to consider myself an athlete. It is worth noting that many experts in the bodybuilding world believe even this level of protein is inadequate for athletes, and possibly for weight loss as well. This is a hot controversy, and certainly, more research is needed to clarify these questions.

The reason I've increased the amount of protein I consume is to try to maintain the muscle I currently have while building additional muscle and boosting fat loss. This important consideration is not often addressed in typical weight loss programs. I've been following this approach for two-and-a-half years now, while closely monitoring my kidney function, and again, I'm living proof that it works.

A word of caution if you are planning on switching to a high-protein diet: If you're over the age of 40, are a diabetic or have other health issues, you should consult with a healthcare professional who will check your kidney function before you adopt a high-protein diet. As you increase your protein, you should continue to check-in with your healthcare professional while you're in the weight-loss program, because high-protein can be hard on your kidneys since that is where it's excreted.

Eating higher protein and lower carbs will also decrease your hunger hormone, Ghrelin, which is pure magic. When you eat protein at least three times a day, this helps maintain a steady blood sugar level, and then you tend to not be as hungry throughout the day because your hormones remain in check. If you crave unhealthy carbs such as donuts, muffins, and other junk food that's around the office or at home, this is an excellent strategy you can use to combat your junk food cravings.

In general, people tend to eat far too many carbohydrates, and too many refined carbohydrates more specifically. Refined carbohydrates, such as white bread and white rice, are quickly digested, but often lack key nutrients that have been removed in processing methods, and therefore are significantly lacking in fiber. This results in a rapid increase in blood sugar often referred to as a spike. It may be an ideal way to achieve a boost prior to a workout, but it's not ideal when ingested alone and when you're sedentary. Whole grains, on the other hand, are less processed, and so are absorbed more slowly, resulting in a more gradual increase in blood sugar and steadier levels. Examples of these foods include whole grain bread, oatmeal (not instant), wild rice and other grains. And when combined with protein, the blood sugar rise is even slower and more gradual.

The ADA recommends two or three servings per day and about 30 grams of carbohydrates in an average serving—which is a small amount compared to what Americans usually eat. The last time you went to a Mexican restaurant, did you notice the rice serving was monstrous? A full serving of rice should be in the range of one-half to three-quarters of a cup. A sweet potato, if that's an option, would be roughly six ounces per 30 grams of carbs. The same applies to a white potato. French fries are off the list, however, because when we eat carbohydrates laden with fat both our fats and carbohydrates are calorically high. Those are two energy sources. That means if we indulge in this manner, more than likely you will exceed your total caloric intake for the day. When this occurs, we tend to store the extra calories as fat.

It's a little unclear as to how many fats per day you should have. Certainly, we want to eat good fats: nuts, avocados, and healthy oils such as olive oil. Consider an approximate range of 30-60 grams per day as a benchmark. That's not much, but it may fluctuate according to each person's needs and their metabolism.

A lot of healthcare professionals are frightened to death of people raising their protein intake to the range of my protein level. They think what competitive athletes do is crazy, and I would ask you to keep an open mind and to understand we can learn a lot from competitive athletes that could enhance our success with weight loss and subsequent maintenance. That's what I've tried to do. I'm in this world now, initially to observe my daughter and support her endeavors as she developed her career in bodybuilding, and now I'm an active participant. We can gain valuable information about what we should and shouldn't do from competitive athletes. We're all here to learn from each other.

CHAPTER 3

Strategies For Nutritional Success

D ID YOU KNOW THAT it takes 20 minutes after eating for our brains to register that we have even eaten? Portion control helps us ensure that we don't consume too many calories before we become satiated. We tend to eat what's on our plate, so it makes sense that limiting our portions, means we will tend to consume fewer calories.

The process of getting in all your nutrients and being precise with your macros, a term referencing the actual grams or ounces of food you consume in different categories, doesn't happen overnight. I fought this whole process tooth and nail. Remember that initially, I wanted to eyeball my portions. Eyeballing your portions isn't as precise, but it's far better than not observing and estimating your portions at all. Becoming precise is a process, so go easy on yourself and your expectations as you practice and learn to apply this concept.

Fortunately, there are plenty of strategies you can implement until you evolve to the point of seeking more precision.

If you don't want to weigh your protein, you can use the visual aid of imagining that the serving is the size of your hand or the size of a deck of cards. That serving will be in the vicinity of four ounces, so it is an effective measuring aide. A double deck of cards is correct for fish and egg whites, because both are very low-calorie, as I've mentioned. This method is especially convenient when you're traveling, and don't have room to pack a food scale and measuring utensils. I always make room, and that's why I travel with a large suitcase.

When eating out, pack half your meal into a to-go container right away, so you're not tempted to consume the entire plate of food. Order a salad with no dressing to eat before the meal, and keep the bread off the table unless you're sure you can control your consumption. Ask your friends and family to help you by ordering healthy meals, and to abstain from ordering foods that will tempt you. It takes a village of support to get started, especially until you're able to gain more control over your choices and temptations.

At home, drink a large glass of water, then have a salad with dressing on the side (only dipping your fork into the dressing) before eating your meal. You might consider eating with a corn cob pick (my favorite), or chopsticks, to slow yourself down. Keep the TV off so you can concentrate on enjoying your meal, and chew fully before swallowing. Enjoy the full sensory experience of eating.

CHAPTER 4

Invisible Calories

JUST AS MEASURING YOUR food is important to ensure precise calculation of your macros (protein, fats, and carbs), it's also important to read the labels of the food you consume. When you do this, you know exactly what you're putting into your body, and can control the portions accordingly.

Reading labels can be quite confusing, especially when you're first starting out. Often, packaged foods have multiple servings in one container, but you might not realize this until you read the label. For example, a bag of chips might look like a small portion, but it could still be more than one serving. Popcorn and soda are notorious for hiding their total servings. Any packaged food label should be analyzed to determine the number of servings and calories. As you become more sophisticated, you can also analyze the macro content for protein, fat, and carbs (total versus net, and fiber content.)

From a health perspective, you want to focus on fat and carbohydrates. You'll also want to pay attention to fiber, and part of the reason why fiber's important is because you don't digest it. Therefore, if a portion of the carbs are fiber, you can remove those carb/fiber (if insoluble) calories from the total calories listed leaving the total net carbs that will be absorbed. Remember, insoluble fiber carbs are removed because you will not absorb these calories.

For example, Quest protein bars are high in protein and fiber. Because the fiber is high, you only absorb five net carbs in a 20-gram protein bar. Fiber can also be extremely satisfying, particularly when you eat a protein bar with a large glass of water. Doing so helps the fiber to expand, and you will find that you feel more satiated. This is why protein bars can be a great meal replacement. However, I always prefer real food whenever possible over even a relatively healthy protein bar that is processed.

We also need to take into consideration how many chemicals are in food, because the more the food has been processed, the more likely that the chemical content will be higher. That's not a great thing for any of us. **When I talk about eating clean, I'm referring to eating as fresh and organic, and unprocessed as possible.**

Getting into the habit of reading the labels will give you more control over your choices, and offer you a better idea if you're making a good decision based on your analysis.

I use the app, MyFitnessPal, because you can truly find any food—whether it's store-bought, or you're dining at a restaurant—within the app. You can even scan the barcode, and the food's macros will automatically populate. Because it performs the calculations for you and shows you the macros, you can educate yourself on what you're putting into your body.

There are many different apps you can use when counting your calories. (See MyFitnessPal in the RESOURCES section.) MyFitnessPal happens to be the one I'm the most familiar with, but you can use any one of the multitudes of apps on the market. The key is to *use these effective new fitness/tracking apps consistently.* Remember, it's better to make the entry before you eat the food, because we conveniently suffer from food recall amnesia after we've eaten. This will derail us if we let it! So, remember all the calories count, even the ones you do not recall.

CHAPTER 5

Calories... Calculating Your Daily Caloric Intake

W HEN I FINALLY HIRED a show coach, I found I wasn't eating enough because I hadn't been listening to my daughter. It was one of those times when it was difficult to hear what she was saying. She'd been telling me I wasn't eating enough, but it was going in one ear and out the other. I'd been so brainwashed over the years into thinking that I needed to consume even fewer calories if I wasn't losing weight, that I refused to hear her. This is what we do in America. You've probably heard the advice: in order to lose weight, you need to "eat less and move more." In my opinion (and based on talking to experts, as well as reading the latest research), it is far more complicated than this trite advice suggests.

One of the first things my show coach told me was, "You've got to eat more." I was instructed to especially eat more around my workouts, and this was a revelation for me as I had been starving myself around workouts. *I'm supposed to eat some carbs before I work out? Party time, that's exciting!* However, my coach clarified quickly that it didn't mean I could have six donuts. He meant only pure carbs such as quick, processed, absorbable carbs that are found in cream of rice, oatmeal, or fruit. Even instant grits will work. That's exactly what I do now before I work out. Even eating carbohydrates *during* the workout if you're lifting weights can make your workout much more effective. You will get stronger more quickly, because muscles love readily available calories in the form of processed, refined carbohydrates before, during, and after workouts. Muscles also love protein in advance of a workout, and also *after* a workout. More new information to learn! My coach boosted my intake of carbohydrates around my workout, as well as my intake of good healthy fats, and protein. Surprise! I began to lose weight again after being at a frustrating plateau for six months. I couldn't believe it, and not surprising, Katherine said, "I told you so."

What happens to many people who are trying to lose weight is they end up eating too few calories. This even applies to people who aren't trying to lose weight, but who may be wondering why they're gaining weight. I hear it typically from healthcare professionals, especially nurse practitioners, who tell me they're so busy they literally don't eat all day long. Then they don't understand why they're not losing weight when they're eating one big meal at night. In fact, they're probably gaining weight.

When you starve your body all day, it reacts by slowing down your metabolism. That's because your body thinks you're a hunter/gatherer, and you've run out of food. The body is trying to conserve energy to endure that famine period. In this situation, the best thing you can do to promote weight loss and weight maintenance is to fuel your furnace throughout the day. We know eating breakfast boosts our metabolism, but make sure you eat lunch, too. If you can eat a healthy, high-protein snack mid-morning and mid-afternoon, that's a metabolic bonus. Eating more frequently fuels your metabolism and keeps your engine revved. I know this advice may come as a shock because it is contrary to popular myth, but it's true! However, there is new information about the benefits of fasting a part of each day (intermittent fasting), but it is beyond the scope of this book to explain this in detail. Also, keep in mind the effectiveness of intermittent fasting is still being studied.

My advice for those who feel they've reached a plateau is to schedule a nutritional consultation with a nutritionist, dietician, trainer or coach who can help you. (Remember, not all trainers are created equal in their knowledge about nutrition). You could also speak to a healthcare professional, like a nurse practitioner, if they have more extensive knowledge than the average nurse practitioner—especially as it pertains to working with weight loss and athletes. If they're in bariatrics, or they specialize in obesity and weight loss, they can likely give sound nutritional advice. But, remember, if you're not successful working with an individual, find someone else. Don't keep beating your head against the wall. (See FINDING THE RIGHT TEAM in the RESOURCES section).

A caution to readers around fruits, and other "healthy foods." These foods can be high in calories, even though they're super healthy for you. The calories can add up quickly, so a great strategy for weight loss, and weight maintenance, is to savor small amounts of fruit. Keep the juices and fresh fruit to a minimum. A little bit goes a long way calorically.

CHAPTER 6

Food Preparation

MANY OF US KNOW what we should do in many cases, and that's part of our reluctance to reach out and ask for help. But we also need to understand that at times it's necessary to use outside help to assist us in achieving our health and fitness goals. We should be willing to seek help and acknowledge and recognize the advantages of asking for and getting help. This is much more productive than feeling as though we have to figure everything out on our own because we're smart, and "should" have the answers to any question or challenge. Food prepping can get complicated if you let it. My goal is to keep these steps simple and to give you a few general guidelines to making healthy living easier. I'm all about pushing the "easy button" whenever possible.

When it comes to grocery shopping— whether you do it yourself, or have someone else do it—you will benefit from using a list. You will also benefit from shopping when you are not hungry. A good habit is to shop around the perimeter, where the fresh foods are usually stocked or located. If you can, stay out of the center aisles where the tempting, processed food tends to be located.

My family usually buys and preps food for a week. It doesn't always stretch that long, but we have a backup freezer for extra fortifications. Since protein is the most time-consuming to cook, the goal should be to have enough prepped to get you through the better part of the week, until you can use another day that's not too crazy and chaotic to food prep again.

I'm a big fan of frozen vegetables that I keep ready to go with the portions of protein that I set out to take with me for the day. You can use just about any vegetable to go with the protein as well as whatever carbohydrates you like. This might be a sweet potato, regular potato, or rice... just be careful about the quantity. Remember a serving is about a half-cup or the size of a lime or large egg. The portion is smaller than most of us think.

Ideally, you want to keep high-glycemic vegetables such as corn and peas to a minimum because they can cause a spike in your blood sugar. It's better to pack green vegetables like lettuce, kale, cucumbers, celery, peppers, green beans, and spinach, that are low-glycemic. Since you can eat more of these, you will feel fuller without the calories adding up.

Even when I am cooking from a recipe, I lean toward simplicity. My idea of a healthy recipe includes a lean protein, maybe seasoned with lemon or lime. Then I add low glycemic vegetables, and less-processed carbohydrates, or a whole grain to the plate. I'm not into fancy because fancy means complicated and potentially time-consuming. It also means hidden calories, and honestly, I like the taste of clean food. I like plain lettuce with no dressing. I didn't always. At one point, I thought it was horrible, but I learned to appreciate how much diet and the success of your eating plan hinges on your mindset. If you can hang in there with your mind, and tell yourself, *I'm going to enjoy the taste of this salad without the dressing obscuring it*, then with time, you will enjoy a salad without anything on it. I don't mind if my salad has any lemon or lime on it. I like the flavor of the lettuces, and I like cucumbers, celery, tomatoes, and onions. I enjoy it now that way, and I get angry when a restaurant salad is delivered to my table, and the server did not hear what I said when I ordered, so they've put cheese and croutons on it, and maybe they've drizzled dressing all over the top—heaven forbid! Five million calories. It's too easy to take a clean-as-a-whistle-low-calorie salad, and turn it into a chicken fried steak equivalent. Restaurants do it all the time.

Getting to this point of simplicity, however, was a long process, and it may take you a while to get there. Don't get discouraged if you find this to be the case. Remember, "TTT," things take time especially, good things, like healthy goals.

I started to enjoy the natural flavors of the salad instead *in order* to make the transition, and so I could more effectively reach my goals. Focusing on those natural sensations became a source of excitement and indulgence for me. **I'm a big fan of phasing out and phasing in changes, and not making dramatic, all-or-nothing decisions.** Because I approached the eating change in this manner, my process took a long time. In fact, it took months and months, and months and months totaling over three years.

Please make sure to give yourself time and to be forgiving with any missteps. You know you can get right back on the horse at anytime, and you don't need to chastise yourself unduly. A key part of your long-term success is working on transforming your negative self-speak to positive self-speak. Focus on eliminating negative words and phrases when referencing yourself (even to yourself.) It matters.

The concept of simple and clean eating is consistent with how I like to live my life, and that is as simple and uncomplicated as possible. It makes sense since I have an addiction to nature and the outdoors. I've learned that part of a simple lifestyle and philosophy means tapping into your gratefulness and being present in what you're doing. You might be mid-conversation with a person and unable to notice the moon, or the flowers on the sidewalk because you're not fully present in the moment. I lived this way for a good portion of my life. If I made a phone call in the great outdoors, I never would've noticed the beautiful moon, trees, or the flowers around me. Now if I'm on a phone call, I like to walk outdoors to embrace the natural environment while conducting business. For me, that's combining the best of both worlds. Give it a try. I love my open-air office.

Simplicity doesn't have to mean deprivation. In fact, simplicity can enhance your life. When you refocus on the joy derived from living a less stressful and less complicated life and eat clean, healthy food you can individually savor, (versus trying to deal with a complicated recipe), you will begin to appreciate the true experience of living and eating.

Section III:
EXERCISE

CHAPTER 7

An "Effective" Exercise Program

I N THIS SECTION, YOU will learn about the life-saving, life-extending, life-enhancing benefits of exercise. I will also discuss the essential components of fitness, different types of exercise, how to get started exercising, and more importantly, how to make it fun!

Finally, I will share my "tried and true" tips and tricks to help you successfully deal with challenges and stumbling blocks.

Challenges invariably arise and threaten to derail us from pursuing our fitness and health goals unless we are prepared.

Physical exercise increases our energy and promotes physical, mental and psychological well-being, and it's a powerful preventative medicine. Exercise not only improves your quality of life but it offers many other benefits. Physical exercise lowers the risk of many health problems including anxiety, cardiovascular disease, back pain, cancers, chronic lung disease, diabetes, obesity, hypertension, and osteoporosis. In fact, did you know weightlifting (also known as resistance training), and walking helps to improve bone density?

Most Americans do not get the recommended amount of exercise.

In fact, according to the CDC;

- Only 51.7 percent of adults 18 years of age and over, met the Physical Activity Guidelines for aerobic physical activity (AKA cardio) of 150 minutes a week.

- Only 21.7 percent of adults 18 years of age and over, met the Physical Activity Guidelines for both aerobic and muscle-strengthening activity.

You can dramatically improve your quality of life by preventing or delaying the development of these various health problems, and you can also improve your day-to-day quality of life. Exercise is a magic bullet, and I believe it is the path to the fountain of youth! I feel and look better at 62 than I did in my thirties.

It's also important to choose exercises that are less likely to cause you injury. If you are older or have a past or current history of injuries or ailments, then you will want to select a type of exercise program that won't aggravate existing problems or cause new problems. You might consider water aerobics or gentle yoga instead of a boot camp or aerobics class.

But what exactly is fitness? Physical fitness is a general state of health and well-being that optimally includes strength, endurance, and flexibility. Often, people emphasize only one or two of these aspects of fitness. For example, runners demonstrate impressive endurance, but many do not possess strength and flexibility. Weightlifters may be strong but lack endurance and occasionally flexibility.

In 2016, The American Heart Association recommended at least 30 minutes of moderate-intensity aerobic activity at least five days a week for a total of 150 minutes to achieve overall cardiovascular health. You can substitute this guideline for 25 minutes of vigorous aerobic activity at least three days a week for a total of 75 minutes. Or, you can apply a combination of moderate and vigorous intensity/aerobic activity and moderate to high-intensity muscle strengthening activity at least two days a week for additional health benefits.

Cardio exercise should be performed for about 30 minutes, five times a week and may include swimming, walking, running, bicycling, elliptical, or the use of a Stairmaster. **Note: swimming and working out on the elliptical machine are not weight-bearing and do not reduce the risk of osteoporosis.**

When performing cardio exercises, it's important to define your target rate. It is recommended that you exercise within 55 to 85 percent of your maximum heart rate for at least 20 to 30 minutes to obtain the best results. Your maximum heart rate is roughly calculated as 220 minus your age. This is the upper limit of what your cardiovascular system can handle during physical activity. There are a variety of heart rate calculators you can access online including the following target heart rate calculator: **active.com/fitness/calculators/heart**. Please make sure you respect the vital recommendation to safely perform cardio exercise without putting yourself at risk.

Resistance training also known as weightlifting, offers many benefits including improving core strength, balance and posture, reducing the risk of back pain, increasing muscle mass and bone density, even tightening skin and reducing cellulite that develops as we age from loss of collagen. I can vouch for many of these benefits having experienced them as a result of losing weight and weightlifting. When I first lost weight, I had lots of loose skin (like a Shar-Pei dog!) but over several years' time that loose skin has tightened up. I did this without surgery, and I feel anytime you can achieve your optimal results without going under the knife, it's a win!

When starting a weight training program, you must learn proper technique and even consider hiring a trainer to teach you how to use the weights properly and to maintain correct form. Taking this precaution will reduce your risk of injury as it increases the benefits you will derive from lifting.

Warming up, cooling down and stretching are also imperative actions you must take when you implement an exercise program or begin to lift weights. Perform stretching exercises between sets of weightlifting exercises, also after you've completed exercise especially if you didn't stretch between sets. If you hire a trainer, they can also help you to learn how to stretch properly because there is a system to applying these correct machinations, especially if you're lifting weights. Strive to do the stretches correlating with the part of your body that you worked out during weightlifting.

What's the real scoop on exercising for weight loss? First, you need to understand you cannot out exercise an unhealthy diet. If you are consuming too many calories and lots of junk food this will make it difficult for you to lose weight. Weight loss requires an integrated approach incorporating nutrition, exercise, mindset, and environment. Exercise alone is unlikely to be effective. Plus, exercise may boost your appetite so be sure to drink extra water, stick to your eating plan, and get plenty of rest.

Before you start exercising, make sure you receive medical clearance, especially if you have any health or medical problems, or if you're over 50 years old.

You may also need help in assessing your fitness level. You can start by choosing an activity and setting a measurable starting goal. Be realistic about your aims. It is far better to start out with the goal of walking 5 to 10 or even 15 minutes a day every day for a week and then reevaluate after a week or two. You can increase your duration and intensity gradually over weeks and months if you're feeling well and not having any severe pain. You may notice minor soreness when you first adjust to your program because your body is not used to the exercise. That's normal, but it should subside over several days. It's also helpful to set a plan using detailed steps. You can make appointments in your calendar noting when you're going to exercise. A strategy I find very helpful is to make appointments with *yourself* using your calendar—either online or using an "old-fashioned" paper calendar/schedule book. You pick the system that will work just for you. You'll note, I talk about doing this multiple times throughout this book. That is because you can use this technique to accomplish many goals on your transformation journey.

If you're struggling to stay motivated, ask yourself what are your stumbling blocks. Try to get to the heart of why you don't want to exercise. Not wanting to fulfill your fitness goals is usually a sign of a bigger challenge, and can always be traced back to your mindset.

Preparation is key in so many aspects of our health program, but it is especially important when it comes to exercise. You can simply walk out the door to exercise, and it takes very little preparation, but if you're going to a gym, it involves more willpower and planning.

Do you need to find a gym? Do you need workout clothes? Do you need shoes? Do you need a water bottle? Do you need to hire a trainer? Do you need to find a workout partner or a group class to join? What do you need to ensure you are prepared?

Don't over analyze or over think your plans, and certainly don't allow yourself to come up with excuses. Nike has the right idea when they say, "Just do it." When you do hold yourself accountable and show up, you can record your exercise in an app or journal that allows you to track your progress over time. You will discover this is very empowering and can provide you with confidence and useful information that you can apply to improve your exercise / fitness program.

It's critical to anticipate barriers and stumbling blocks that may arise. How can you deal with these barriers? Who can help you work through these barriers and challenges? Who is in your support system? Can you add people to your support system to grow a village of support? The more support you create for yourself, the more potential you will have for success and reaching your goals.

Ask yourself these pivotal questions to invigorate your challenge: What is one exercise goal you would like to accomplish this week? What small concrete task can you do this week to move forward toward achieving your exercise goals? Make that one thing, easy and doable so you can't help but succeed. This will build your momentum, and you will feel very good about yourself.

Now, go to it!

Is Your Cardio Regimen Helping Or Hurting You?

Cardio is important, but it's *not* the one-and-only solution to weight loss. If taken out of the context of moderation, it can, in fact, be harmful to your journey. As I said before, you cannot out-exercise an unhealthy diet. This is one of my favorite sayings because it is TRUE! My daughter often reminds me of this fact.

Even as much as two hours of cardio a day will not contribute to weight loss as much as what we eat does. Eighty percent of weight loss success is directly related to what we eat. Only a small proportion is related to exercise. However, our efforts to lose weight can backfire if we exercise too much. This is because too much exercise can stress out our bodies. When your body is stressed out, it raises its cortisol levels, our stress hormone. This, in turn, contributes to the body storing more fat, and to the additional plateauing of weight loss and in some cases, even cause weight gain.

I'm walking proof of this. At first, I ate 1,200 calories a day. At the gym, I would crank out serious cardio, at least an hour a day and sometimes more than that. I was keeping my heart rate way up, and I was weightlifting, and this eventually wore me out. Then I found I was stuck because I wasn't eating enough calories to support so much exercise. In short: I was stressing my body out. It wasn't until I received significant nutritional assistance from both Kat and my show trainer that my weight started to drop again. The bottom line is, we do need to be careful. Less may be more when it comes to exercise, but the same may not hold true for your calorie intake. *Eat more, move less* may be more accurate than the adage *eat less, move more*. That's pretty counterintuitive!

When my show coach (and nutritional advisor) started working with me, he told me I was doing too much cardio, and gave me a new exercise program. I felt much better quickly, more relieved and relaxed, and I discovered the program was more doable than I thought. As I continued, my efforts became easier because of his advice and new program, nutritionally, physically and mentally speaking. My coach helped me to understand the importance of staying mellow, and of not being too anxious. That's important because often we're in an anxious state when we're trying to lose weight. *When can I weigh myself? Oh no, I weighed myself two days in a row, and I haven't lost anything. This program's not working*! We panic and overreact. And then our cortisol levels go up and guess what—our weight loss stalls out.

Try to remember that weight isn't linear. Daily weights don't necessarily correlate with food consumption from the day before. It's more complex than that. It's better to compare week-to-week or even month-to-month over time. Day-to-day is *not* reliable and can be intensely discouraging and de-motivating.

It's Time To Find Some Balance.

The American Heart Association's recommendation for cardio is about 150 minutes of moderate exercise per week. (See Cardio Recommendations in RESOURCES). The great news is you can do it in bits and pieces. Twenty minutes a day if you're dedicated to daily gym sessions, 40 minutes each time if you can only make it a few days a week. We really don't have to do hours of exercise, plus cardio, every single day. I'm learning this. Now, I average 30 minutes of cardio per day, in addition to weightlifting for 30-60 minutes depending on the specific workout program and muscle group I'm focusing on that day. And now I take every third day off from weightlifting to give my body some extra rest and recovery time.

When I'm traveling, I can reduce my time by doing High Intensity Interval Training (HIIT)—one minute at max heart rate, one minute slower, one minute at max, one minute at a slower rate. Sometimes, I can work through my program in 12 to 20 minutes if my heart rate stays elevated for the right duration of time. You don't need massive amounts of time to work on your cardio. It's more important to reduce your stress and monitor your cortisol levels to ensure your body is working in sync to support your goals, instead of fighting your body.

CHAPTER 8

Going Solo Is A No-No

I'VE FOUND THAT WHEN you pay for services, there is more accountability, and you're more likely to listen to the advice you've been given. You listen more than when a friend tries to help you—or even worse, a family member gives you advice. Which means there's more accountability, and ultimately more learning, and that leads to greater progress toward your goals.

You also tend to be more motivated when you hire an expert, and you pay for their services. You've got skin in the game, and you don't want to disappoint your trainer or coach. This type of relationship is powerful. If you think you can't afford these services, sure, maybe you can't afford it every week, but you might be able to afford it once a month. You will find even limited time with a trainer is priceless in terms of the benefits for you.

When a family or close friend is helping you attain your fitness goals, we put up resistance. Katherine loves to point this out to me. As an example, she would often ask what I had learned after I'd met with my show coach. Once I'd responded she would typically say, "I told you that months ago, but you didn't hear it." The risk of working with loved ones is that we will resist their best intentions and so we will not be open to what they try to tell us.

CHAPTER 9

Respecting Your Cortisol Levels

W E KNOW ELEVATED CORTISOL levels correlate with high levels of stress, but the signs
can be a little tricky to diagnose—feeling anxious, not sleeping, maybe even feeling your heart-rate going fast when it shouldn't be, and having a low amount
of energy. It's all about reducing stress. When we reduce
stress, we reduce the amount of cortisol in our bodies, too
and that may help you to both lose weight and feel better.

The right amount of cardio and the right amount of exercise should be energizing to us, not exhausting. If we're
finding that as we exercise more, we're worn to the bone,

it's probably an indicator we're either not eating enough, and/or we're doing too much exercise. If you're experiencing this sign, it's a good idea to consult with a trainer or nutritional expert. As a nurse practitioner, I know enough to manage the basics of our patients' medical problems, but I don't have the knowledge and expertise that coaches, trainers, and dieticians possess. I'm guessing whether you are a nurse practitioner or not; you likely don't have the depth of knowledge of these specialists.

The Benefits Of Having A Trainer

A good trainer is worth their weight in gold and worth every penny you pay them. They will provide you with expertise and guidance, teaching and monitoring how you perform your exercises, helping you to prevent injuries, advising on nutrition, lifestyle, stress, weight loss—you name it. They will also provide you with a system of accountability, which can be the difference between achieving your goals and coming up short. Finally, they can provide you with a source of emotional support that can be very affirming. Having a person in your life who knows and shares in your health and fitness-related struggles and victories is priceless.

This is what I have found.

Keep in mind, I never worked with a trainer until three years ago, despite having exercised and attempts to stay healthy my entire life. I did not know what I was missing.

In addition, this might have been a missing link and a big reason for my lifetime of yo-yoing with my weight. Now, I'd rather pay for coaching than buy a new dress or have my nails done. How about that?

Section IV:
MINDSET

CHAPTER 10

Mindset Is Everything

A STANFORD UNIVERSITY IQ VERSUS Attitude Study suggests that our attitudes are a better predictor of our success than our intelligence. Years ago, Henry Ford proposed a similar concept, when he said, "Whether you think you can or you think you can't, you are right."

This statement is why a positive, "can do" attitude is the key to your success and achieving your goals. It is the driver behind everything else you do!

According to Stanford University researcher Carolyn Dweck, there are two types of mindsets or basic core attitudes people possess. The first is a fixed mindset. People with this type of mindset believe they really can't change, are often very set in their ways and are afraid to try new things.

The second type of mindset is a growth mindset. People with this type of mindset believe that with effort and practice they can change and grow. They embrace challenges as opportunities to learn to try something new. They see failure as information to learn from and an opportunity to devise a new strategy or approach to address that challenge. As Emma Goldman, a famous feminist, once said, "Failure is Impossible." This is precisely how people with a growth mindset think.

It's not surprising to learn then, that people possessing a growth mindset outperform people with a fixed mindset even if they have a lower IQ.

What type of mindset do you use to govern your life?

Mindset and attitude are everything. When we tap into our intuition, self-awareness, and mental positivity, we develop insight into our thoughts, and more control over them as well. These new improved thoughts create new improved feelings that result in new improved behaviors. Then guess what happens? We create a new improved self—voila! We transform ourselves. How cool is that? If you want to do great things in life, if you want to accomplish your wildest dreams, you need to work on your mindset, your attitudes, your core beliefs, and your perspective on life. Everything about the success we reach in life is related to our thoughts, attitudes, and beliefs. When we tap into absolute positivity, we develop feelings that then result in our behaviors.

Our minds cannot tell the difference between what's real and imaginary. If we can learn to change or shift our negative thoughts to positive ones, then we can set in motion a mental habit that can transform our lives.

Unless we have cleaned our inner house, we have no hope of accomplishing our goals and dreams. This is hard work. If we do accomplish our goals, they may not be sustainable because we have not addressed our inner thoughts, attitudes, and beliefs. For a sustained transformation, we need to clean our inner house and then keep it clean.

Are you a glass half empty or a glass half full person?

If you find yourself eating a lot of junk food when you are stressed it may be worthwhile to stop and think about what feelings are behind your behavior. Look deeper at your thoughts? Do you feel unworthy? Do you feel unhealthy, unattractive, unlovable? Do you lack confidence? Is this why you are feeling bad about yourself, and perhaps that's why you are eating junk food?

Remember, your thoughts become you! This is all we really have. We are our thoughts. If you want to improve your life, you need to take control of your thoughts. As James Redfield says, "Where attention goes, energy flows." We must learn to be laser-focused on our goals if we want to achieve them. However, this takes practice, so be patient with yourself.

You also need to think about who you associate with as well. Do you have friends who are positive or negative? It's important to identify these traits because they have a major influence on your thoughts, attitudes, feelings, and behavior, too. The saying, "Pick your friends carefully," is very true.

Mind Over Matter

My perception of *mind over matter* is different from the standard interpretation. I believe our minds dictate our behaviors and actions. When our mindset is positive, self-aware, goal-oriented, and focused- we tend to make decisions and develop habits and behaviors that benefit our physical health.

I believe that the more insight and awareness we have into our thoughts, the more that will impact our behavior by changing our feelings. Our thoughts dictate our feelings, which leads to our day-to-day behaviors.

If you don't take the inner journey and slay your dragons, you're not going to be able to make changes in your behaviors and habits, especially sustained changes over time.

Let's think about using a different reward system for ourselves. Our culture has taught us to reward ourselves by perpetually eating, right? We eat when we are sad. We eat when we are glad. We eat when we have no idea how we are feeling. We just eat.

Have you ever stopped to consider if the reward system you were culturally raised with is really serving your goals, serving where you want to be and where you want to go in your life?

As Katherine explains, "You can't hate yourself thin. You have to learn how to love and respect yourself, and work through some of that emotional baggage to enable committing fully to—and be successful in—making healthy, sustained lifestyle changes."

Here's an example of how I had to change my habits and improve them in order to take care of myself, especially when traveling. I needed to be satisfied in terms of dealing with my hunger and challenges, and not feel as though I was withholding anything from myself. One of the only ways I could accomplish this was to stash pre-packed protein snacks in my computer bag for quick and easy access. When I first started this journey, I would have perceived my dietary changes as total deprivation. Now, I know that making healthy decisions is serving me. It's serving my goals, and it's making me feel good about myself. I want a healthy body, and the only way I'm going to have a healthy body is to feed it what it can maximally benefit from on a consistent, regular basis.

Interestingly, discipline comes from insight and awareness around what's going on in our heads.

The body changes you might experience are a nice result of the mind work, but there's bodywork involved, too.

Honestly, and in my experience, you develop so much more discipline from a balanced mind, a mind that has looked into itself.

My new motto is "No Excuses." I identify with this saying so strongly because I used to have a million excuses, and they were all very convincing. I would say to myself; *I need my rest. I need eight hours of sleep every night. I won't be able to think if I don't get my rest. I'll get sick if I don't get my rest.*

Sometimes it's the little voice inside our heads that doesn't want to change. Because change is uncomfortable.

I'm an advocate of clearing and quieting our minds.

Everyone's going to have a different solution for quieting their mind. Ask yourself what do you need to do to calm your mind?

We often hold the carrot out to ridiculous lengths because our lists are so long, and our email never ends. What are we trying to do to ourselves? The strategy should be to slow our lives down. Don't be afraid to look at your thoughts and feelings. And don't be afraid of the process involved in developing discipline and daily strength to stay the course. Slow, sustained changes over time will lead to accomplishing your goals. This also applies to developing a positive attitude, and a focused and peaceful mind. I am a work in progress, too, as I still stress out, lose focus and have my negative moments. But I have a lot more awareness, and that is key to transforming yourself and your life.

Slaying Your Dragons AKA Inner Gremlins (Inner Critique)

Gremlins are our biggest dream busters! They are the voices in our heads that tell us we can't do something (that we want to do.) They come up with a million reasons why we should not do something. They try to derail us when we begin a new healthy habit or start working toward a goal. They tell us we are not worthy, we are not smart enough, we don't have the time or money to accomplish our goals, and they even shout at us that we are lazy! Each of us has certain gremlins that rear their ugly heads when we attempt to change our lives for the better. They want us to stay the same, and they will fight with us to convince us that we should not do whatever it is that we have set out to do. It might be to lose weight, change our diets, find a new job, go back to school, get a divorce, or any other goal or dream you want to pursue.

The way to manage gremlins is to acknowledge them. Just notice them. Do not engage gremlins because they will give you more reasons why you should not change. They will undermine your best intentions. However, they lose power when we simply say, "OK, I hear what you are saying but I am not going to give in to what you are saying about me. In fact, what you are saying is NOT true." Remind yourself that you are smart and competent and can accomplish your goals.

You will think what the gremlin is saying is true, but you must fight that inclination and realize if you are feeling bad that is probably a gremlin speaking to you. It is probably a gremlin trying to undermine your confidence and future actions and success.

Awareness and insight are keys to slaying your gremlins. However, the most effective way to silence gremlins is to take action. Even small steps will quiet the gremlins. You may notice as you take action this happens.

The other technique that is helpful in managing gremlins is to keep your eye on the prize! In other words, remember your goal and what it is that you want. Vividly imagine what it's going to feel like, look like and taste like when you reach your goal. Keep those images in your head and understand that gremlins are just a natural part of any change. The bigger the change, the louder the gremlins are going to scream. This is because they are in charge of maintaining the status quo and if you rock the boat, they will let you know it. Rock the boat anyway because this is the only way you will reach your dreams.

I rocked my gremlins' boat big time when I decided to return to school to earn my doctorate at 59 years old. Who does that? My gremlins went crazy telling me all the reasons I would not succeed: I wasn't smart enough, organized enough, young enough, blah, blah, blah. I had to work intensively with my life coach to gain insight and to learn how to cope with these gremlins, and it worked! Slowly, I became less fearful and began to trust I would be successful.

The same thing happened when I decided to be in my first body building show the following year (after I graduated.) My gremlins were out of control! But as I progressed in my preparation for the show, actually believing I'd be ready to step on stage and not make a fool out of myself, my gremlins began to quiet down. Action, confidence, and competence will eventually quiet the most outspoken gremlins.

Rick Carson, author of *Taming Your Gremlins,* posits that there is "A surprisingly simple method for getting out of your own way." To learn more about this fascinating subject, check out his book.

CHAPTER 11

Resistance To Change

A S HUMANS, WE RESIST change because there's a part of our psyche that wants to stay the same. Dr. James Prochaska, a notable leader in the behavioral field and the first psychologist to win a Medal of Honor for Clinical Research from the American Cancer Society, conducted a study that confirms what we all know to be true: most humans resist change. It's a fact. (See American Cancer Society in RESOURCES).

You have to anticipate your mind is not going to receive these changes with an open heart right away. There is likely going to be resistance to the changes you want to make. If you pour milk into your coffee or tea in the morning, and then someone suggests you measure the milk, it's inconvenient. It makes you upset. Or, maybe you've started going to the gym. Well, there are always good reasons NOT to go to the gym. You get out of work late; you don't want to get up early in the morning; you're not a morning person; you're not an evening person...you can find a thousand, million, zillion excuses. Those excuses can be boiled down to one thing: resistance to change. In the beginning, at least, you're going to be uncomfortable. Your discomfort will continue acutely for several days, if not several weeks, and maybe even longer. Remember that it takes anywhere from two weeks to two months to break an unhealthy habit or establish a new healthy habit. The discomfort will lessen, with practice and with experience, but you have to ride it out to establish new, positive habits. To change, we must get out of our comfort zone, as hard as it is.

Persist. It will get easier. In fact, discipline is only required in the beginning when we are creating a new habit. Once the new habit is a habit (1- 2 months), then it's much easier because we are automated by then! Successful people focus on developing select habits that will ensure their success.

See my section on habits for more detail on how to create new healthy habits and break unhealthy ones.

When I talk about mindset and the natural inclination to resist change, I am not including addictions. Addictions are a whole other kettle of fish and in a league of their own in terms of resistance to change. If you feel like something has power over you, particularly certain foods (or alcohol and/or drugs) that may be a sign that an addiction is involved (or that you have an addiction.) In this case, you will probably need professional help. When it comes to addictions, mind over matter just doesn't work. You can access resources to get help with addictions from a healthcare provider such as a nurse practitioner, or from certain organizations. (See RESOURCES for organizations).

My personal experience popped up early in the process. Resistance reared its ugly head. Katherine kept encouraging me to record my food, and I didn't want to because I thought it would be too much work and would cause me great angst.

Initially, I had trouble locating food entries in the MyFitnessPal app. To make it more fun, Katherine and I would have contests to see who could look up the food entries the fastest. And guess what? She would always find them first. I would get so frustrated. Sometimes, I'd find an incorrect entry that I thought I could get by with, but she'd catch me—she has that capability—and she'd be emphatic about correcting me, "That is *not* the right entry. Check the macros, that's not right!" Remember, **everything is hard until it is easy**. That's just the way it is. So, persevere. It will get easier.

In the beginning, I was a fast eater, and this was severely impacting my progress. I was eating too many calories because I was eating too fast, but it was hard to teach myself how to slow down. After all, I'm a nurse and have been eating on the run pretty much my entire career. That's what we do. But if I was going to be successful, I needed to figure out some way of slowing myself down. So, when I was at home, I started using a corn cob pick as a fork. I'd peck at my food—similar to using chopsticks; except I was using a corn cob pick. Chopsticks are a great tool to help slow you down, too. I posted a picture of myself using the corn cob pick on Facebook, and people thought it was hilarious. But it works! Often, you have to be creative, and do whatever it takes.

I couldn't do a lot of cardio at one time when I was first getting started either, and to be honest, I didn't want to. It was hard to get motivated and to build my stamina. I had the worst time working up to an hour of cardio. It was a big victory when I finally reached 30 minutes. When I first started, it seemed every hotel gym was boiling hot. I was convinced I was going to die each time I went to the gym. I compare it to hot yoga; only it was cardio. I reached the point where I would walk to the front desk, and beg them to have the maintenance person adjust the temperature. As I reflect on this experience, I realize a part of my frustration with the gym temperature was my resistance to change and wanting to find reasons (excuses) to give up.

Eventually, I asked one of my business colleagues if she would text me while I was at the gym to encourage me to keep going. Her texting helped a lot by providing support, encouragement, and accountability. It motivated me. As we developed this habit over time, she'd text me: "Go, Mimi, go!" She jokes that "GoMimiGo" is a new word in her vocabulary.

As long as I'm being honest, I'll admit that I did a fair amount of crying in the beginning when I was adjusting to all these changes. It was weird. I don't cry much now, but I remember looking up at my daughter one day as she was standing in the kitchen, and I sobbed, "My life's over! I can't do all this! I feel like a diabetic, I'm not on medicine, but I feel like a diabetic. My whole world is structured! I can't have chocolate chips anymore! I can't have donuts anymore! I can't have ice cream anymore!" On and on. I couldn't stop crying. In those moments, I genuinely thought my life as I had known it, was over. It was an intensely real moment I had to get through.

And guess what? My life as I knew it was over. I was adopting new habits and a new way of living healthy, and I am planning to sustain these changes for the rest of my life. So, my former way of living and eating is over, and it was over then. Maybe at that point when I had this huge meltdown- at some deeper level I knew it. I was mourning for my past life that I would hopefully never go back to.

Success has a great deal to do with planning and preparation. If evenings are not an ideal time for you to do food prep, then maybe you do it in the morning. Or maybe have your conversations and quality time with your family on the weekends, rather than during weekday evenings. So, maybe weekends would be better for your food prep. Maybe you need to simplify evenings for yourself; have conversations to create the conditions, the structure, and the acceptance you need so your home environment can be a safe place for you after work. Wouldn't that be a nicer alternative than walking into a landmine at the end of a busy day? Even children can be involved in this planning process.

Maybe you hire some help in the evening for a couple of hours, even if it's just a high school student at minimum wage. There are plenty of food prep services available, and numerous grocery stores offer delivery services, so you don't have to waste precious time roaming aisles and driving across town. Buying chopped-up, pre-cooked chicken or other protein in packs as a backup to your meal prep is always a time-saver.

You can hire someone to clean your house, too. Maybe not once a week, but every other month. Houses do not need to be cleaned every week, contrary to popular mother mythology. I don't know about you, but my parents had us do chores every Saturday morning; our house had to be clean. Having a clean house is not a huge priority for me. This is because I live a very busy life with nearly weekly business travel. It seems like I'm either packing or unpacking. I'd rather be at the gym, prepping food, or spending quality time with my family or friends.

A big part of accepting change is telling yourself you need to get over the guilt of feeling like you have to be everything to everyone under all circumstances. I still have thoughts that I should spend every free moment with my aging mother. Or, I should be doing this or that, and *what am I doing spending time at the gym on my own? I can't do that!* Oh, my goodness! We forget that we really can't take care of others if we aren't taking care of ourselves. The saying goes, "you can't serve others from an empty vessel." If you deprive yourself to serve others, you will be at risk of becoming angry, frustrated, resentful and stressed out. It's vital to make time and space for the things that keep you healthy and happy in life.

CHAPTER 12

The Five-Second Rule

WE'RE TALKING ABOUT THE Five-Second Rule in this chapter because five seconds is the amount of time you have to act on (or not act on) a health-focused intention (an action) before your mind begins to talk you out of it. Everyone can relate to this dilemma. I'm sure there have been times when you were planning to take a walk, go to the gym, to make a healthy decision about what you're going to eat when suddenly your mind took over and talked you out of your healthy intention! The problem is your mind provides you with highly convincing rationale. You must accept that this is another instance of your gremlins speaking to you, trying to maintain your status quo. As I've mentioned, gremlins are your dream busters! They are the voices inside your head that do NOT want you to change. They do NOT want you to improve your life. They certainly do NOT want you to reach your goals. Making progress toward your goals means you will change and gremlins want you to keep your life exactly as it is, familiar and unchanging. Whenever you meet resistance to change, consider reviewing my section on gremlins.

Also, it is important to practice your health-related actions with urgency and expediency. The more you hesitate and dawdle, the more likely you are to violate the Five-Second Rule. Then look out, you'll be sabotaged. Respect the **Five-Second Rule**, and you will be more likely to succeed in transforming your life one healthy decision at a time.

CHAPTER 13

Setting Goals And Establishing Healthy Habits

"We are what we repeatedly do. Excellence, therefore, is not an act but a habit." ~**Aristotle**

CREATING NEW HEALTHY HABITS or breaking unhealthy habits requires specific skills and strategies to be successful. It is not as simple as just making a change or having more willpower, even though we hear this supposed logic all the time. It is just not true, and I believe this is why most people fail at achieving New Year's resolutions.

If you are not "all in" mentally, then it will be much more challenging for you to commit to what is required to be successful. You will especially be more likely to throw in the towel when the going gets rough. Are you just interested in achieving a certain goal or are you 100 percent committed to that goal?

Goals

It is also critically important to keep your goals in the forefront of your mind and to break down your goals into doable chunks or steps. This is called reverse engineering, meaning, working backward from your goal to your present situation—and then breaking that goal down into achievable steps. What do you need to accomplish today, this week, this month, to reach your goal in one year?

For example, if you want to lose 25 pounds in a year's time, how much do you need to lose per week to reach that goal?

Divide 25 pounds by 52 weeks, and it's approximately a half a pound per week. This is how much you will need to plan to lose per week to reach your goal. Does that seem achievable? Does that seem possible?

How many calories do you need to reduce in your daily food intake and/or how much more exercise do you need to complete to achieve your goal?

Habit Stacking

James Clear developed the concept of habit stacking. Habit stacking is one of the easiest ways to begin a new healthy habit. It is based on associating/attaching the new habit with an existing habit. If your existing habit is always brushing your teeth in the morning and at night, and one of your goals is to drink more water, you would apply the principle of habit stacking in the following way: You could drink a glass of water before or after you brush your teeth. To increase the probability of making that change, you might even pour your glass of water the night before and place it next to your toothbrush. Another example of habit stacking would be to place a full glass of water next to medications or supplements that you take in the morning or evening or both. You can increase your chances of being successful in adopting a new habit by "stacking" it onto an established habit. This is a very effective strategy for developing new habits.

What other habits do you have that you can use to help you progress? For example, what new habit can you stack onto your "drive to work"?

Maybe your goal is to improve your nutrition by increasing your protein intake. How about drinking a protein drink on your way to work and maybe on the way home, too? These are great examples of habit stacking opportunities. Always think, small and achievable. Then pat yourself on the back and tell yourself: "great job!"

The key to habit stacking is to take advantage of what you're already doing because that's going to increase the likelihood you will succeed with a new habit if you associate it with an existing habit.

Small, Easy Changes: Habits

The idea behind making small, easy changes is to set accomplishable and attainable goals. You want to make these shifts in your life so doable you're guaranteed to succeed. Set yourself up for success. When you do this, and when you hit your targets it gives you a sense of accomplishment. Winning will build your confidence, and it will help you to more quickly reach your goals because you are tangibly moving forward.

Small achievable, consistent changes lead to huge changes over time. I can vouch for that fact.

I began my journey by making small consistent changes. I didn't at the time think they would add up too much. Examples for me included drinking more water, eating more protein, getting more sleep, increasing my daily exercise (reducing my stress), calculating invisible calories, preparing my food for the next day, preparing my food for the next week, preparing my food for travel, and recording everything I put in my mouth into my fitness app.

Initially, my changes were very small. I began by drinking more water when I brushed my teeth. I drank more water before, during and after I ate. I went to sleep 15 minutes earlier than normal and set an alarm so I would do it!

Another effective strategy that I've found and that might work for you, too, is to make appointments with yourself. Schedule time to go to the gym, to do your food prep or to go to sleep earlier. This form of habit stacking works because if you always keep appointments (for example, medical appointments), then making appointments for other reasons, particularly for self-care, might also work.

Rather than leaving activities to random times—because we all know how days get busy and the next thing you know you didn't get to your top priorities—block specific time for particular activities, and I bet you will keep your appointments!

Write down the existing habit that you can stack onto the new one. Can you visualize accomplishing this new habit every day for the next week? OK, you are on your way to learning the new skill of habit stacking. Oh, the places you will go and the goals you will accomplish. You will be amazed, and the best part is that it is so easy.

CHAPTER 14

The 24-Hour Solution

2 4-HOUR SOLUTION (CREATING THE OPTIMAL LIFESTYLE TO ACHIEVE GOALS) is made up of three concepts that Coach Kat and I regularly use with our clients, and that they have found life-changing.

1. Fail to Prepare. Prepare to Fail.

I live by this quote, and it's absolutely true. When I'm too tired, and I'm not committed, I don't prepare—which is a set-up for failure. After looking back on the days that I haven't been too successful in my journey, I've realized my failures have usually been precipitated by being unprepared. Part of the preparation process involves scheduling what you need to get done. Make everything about your goal reaching, as easy as possible, so you have no excuses due to not having the tools you need to succeed. (You can apply this strategy to food prep. You need to plan what you will eat and when you will eat).

We're so good about scheduling other things in our lives—scheduling meetings with people for work or school, a hair appointment, taking our car to be fixed. However, often we don't think to schedule our time at the gym, or to schedule a call with a trainer. All the pieces of meeting our own needs should be scheduled so we will make sure they happen. Just as we would do with a doctor's appointment or nurse practitioner's appointment, if we aren't able to make that appointment then we need to reschedule it right away.

If we're scheduled to go exercise right after work, but there's no way we can do it because we had to stay late at work, our exercise time must get rescheduled right away. As soon as possible, in fact. If we're food prepping, we should schedule when it's going to be done. It works best when you put the appointment right in your calendar. When are you going to grocery shop? When are you going to prep your food? Block that time off on your calendar, so you don't overcommit yourself.

Food prep is its own sort of universe in this way. It involves many steps, including grocery shopping (that's another experience that we have to learn how to manage), cooking and preparing the food, and portioning it into ready-to-go meals. It can be a time-consuming process. This is all part of planning, and that involves scheduling. So, take it from me and schedule your food prep.

Even schedule your time with friends, so you make sure it happens. I think part of why people are so connected on Facebook is there's very little accountability today. Facebook was created to enhance in-person connectivity, and instead, we have fewer in-person interactions than ever before. What we may not know is that if you connect to people in person, it will raise your oxytocin—your feel-good hormone. Even though Facebook has monopolized so much of our time, we can still schedule time with our friends and loved ones to stimulate the production of that feel-good hormone.

Often, when we're stressed out, time with friends and family is one of the first things to go. It certainly was for me. The busier we get, the more it's critically important to schedule date time with your friends and loved ones. Otherwise, we end up disconnected from them, and that distance can lead to a huge abyss, which may or may not be remediable. In addition, self-imposed loneliness can contribute to the risk of developing anxiety and depression. Resolving these situations is all a part of extreme self-care. I'm scheduling time with trainers, scheduling time to work out with a buddy at the gym, scheduling date nights with my husband, scheduling time with my daughter, and scheduling time for food prep. When I do this, I make sure all the important aspects of my life get attention.

Operating your life in this manner may seem extremely inconvenient, but it pays off in huge dividends because you've created an accountability plan. You're working out with a friend; you're connecting with that friend; you're building support. You can even develop an agreement with that friend where perhaps you help each other resist trigger foods or trigger situations. Support of this magnitude can make-or-break reaching your goals. Keep in mind; it's a process: phasing out the old friends, phasing in the new friends—unless you can get the old friends on your side.

2. Make Small, Easy Changes

We've covered making small, easy changes as it pertains to transitioning to new habits, and this recommendation is also a part of our 24-Hour Solution. That's how impactful it is! We've added it into our coaching program. Success breeds success and biting off more than you can chew can backfire. When your life becomes stressful, you may lose your ability to maintain too many changes. You might then feel like a failure and have negative thoughts about your ability to accomplish your goals.

When you experience success, congratulate yourself. Celebrate even the smallest achievement. Say you drank a full glass of water this morning when you brushed your teeth. Take a moment to give yourself some kudos. You did it!

Too often, we only praise ourselves when we have done something that we perceive as being big enough to celebrate. And that's not right. When you celebrate even your smallest achievements, you will build your confidence, and a positive mindset/attitude. You will build your belief that you can achieve your goals. Most importantly, you will be building momentum to achieve even more success.

3. Take Imperfect Action Now

You must take action! Even imperfect action is better than inaction. One of the problems we have as humans is that we have an uncanny way of putting things off. We say to ourselves *tomorrow, next week, next month, next year.*

We repeat to ourselves; *it's not a good time right now.* Or, we'll tell ourselves we haven't researched the topic enough. We don't have all the information we need get started. Our brains get so caught up in all the details it cripples us and stops us from acting. Has this ever happened to you?

The way to combat this tendency is to take imperfect action. Once you get started often, you can't figure out what to do next, but that's OK. Even that very small action propels you forward and builds your momentum for more imperfect action and success!

Try it! I think you will be surprised at how effective this approach is in helping you reach your goals.

CHAPTER 15

Pulling The Trigger On Triggers And Addictions

FIRST OF ALL, TRIGGERS derail us. They are like gremlins because their sole purpose is to keep us from achieving our goals. So, triggers must be respected, and we need to develop a way to cope with them. They're the main reason why most people fall off their program. There are three different types of triggers I've defined: trigger foods, trigger people, and trigger situations.

Trigger foods are foods that lead you down a slippery slope. For me, nuts can be a trigger food. Peanut butter can be a trigger food. I have to be really careful that a few nuts won't lead me to abuse them. Because one handful is good, and more handfuls are even better. One tablespoon of peanut butter (95 calories) is good, but more is even better. Triggers tend to be ongoing. These are foods that push our excess buttons; meaning, we can't control the quantity, and it's hard to shut them down.

In some cases, triggers may be related to addictions. If you find that certain foods are controlling you—you're not controlling them—that could indicate an addiction.

I think there's a milder version of attachment to food than addiction, too. With an addiction, the trigger has total control over you. You don't have any control over it. It takes over your life. But there's a continuum where you may feel like you're unable to control quantity, yet it's not a full addiction. I don't feel like I have to go to Overeaters Anonymous because I have a few issues managing the quantity of nuts I eat. It isn't taking control of my entire lifestyle. I can put them away if I put my mind to it.

You may want to keep triggers out of your environment until you feel like you can control them again. Although, it is possible that you might not feel like you will ever be able to control them. When I was first reconstructing my life, I asked my husband not to buy ice cream. I couldn't have it in the freezer because I was used to having it every single night. Not much, but a little. He'd have a huge bowl, and I'd have a little bowl. But it didn't serve me because I kept gaining weight.

I asked him to put my triggers out in the garage some-where—out of sight, out of mind—so I wouldn't be able to access the food I considered trouble for me easily. Whether it was bread, or donuts, or pies, or dessert, or ice cream, butter, jam, nuts, chocolate bits and other candies, or any of those things I might dip into—especially at night—it all went into the garage. I recently asked him, "How tough was it not being able to have any of your goodies around?" He said it was very tough, that it actually had made him angry. He had felt like I didn't want him in the house—and that was honestly quite true. In the early phases of my transformation, I would become pretty irritated that he could eat anything he wanted, yet I couldn't. It continues to be a challenge for both of us.

Trigger people, on the other hand, are folks who for whatever reason do not help you stay on your program. My husband is a classic trigger person because he doesn't really care what he eats. He eats pretty healthily most of the time, but he loves cheese and crackers, ice cream, cookies, cake, and all the goodies I've been trying to mini-mize—if not eliminate—in my own life.

Trigger people don't necessarily bring out the best in you. In fact, without even knowing it they can potentially derail you from staying on your program. You may have trigger friends, and when you go out to eat they might say, "Oh, we don't get together all that often! Here, have some alcohol, and dessert; have whatever you want on the menu. Let's celebrate!" This is a stark contrast to a true friend who's going to help you stay on your program. *That* person might say to you, "You pick the restaurant." When they make that gesture, it gives you the opportunity to pick the restaurant that has calorie counts on the menu. Then you can order and eat clean. You can ask your friends for help in staying away from foods that cause you issues. Maybe you can negotiate with them to not bring bread to the table, or to skip dessert, or that they could order sweet potato fries (one of my favorite foods) instead of triggering French fries.

Just because *you're* developing awareness, doesn't mean anyone else in your world is. That's why we must learn ways to cope with trigger people. You have to learn to depend on yourself in this manner and to plan for those situations that will throw you off your game.

I'm learning you cannot have a conversation with a trigger person, or a loved one when you're upset. You've got to calm yourself down and pick a time when you think they may be open to conversation. Try to be as constructive and positive in your interactions with the person as possible. I'm still not good at holding these conversations with my husband and loved ones. But I am learning the heat of the moment is not the time to have a knock-down-drag-out, angry interaction, because it's going to move you nowhere but backward in the relationship. The person you're talking to is not going to become more open-minded or learn anything from your frustration and anger. Once you're out of control, put yourself in a time-out, and remind yourself it's not the time to have the conversation. As you strive to develop healthier habits, this may be an area in which you will need to learn self-restraint.

You also need to avoid trigger situations. Trigger situations are a setup for failure, for losing your wheels. Anytime you're drinking alcohol, and there's food involved, that's a trigger situation because alcohol consumption leads to impaired inhibitory control, as detailed in a 2015 research study published in *Health Psychology*. (To access the full article, see REFERENCES).

Going on a cruise is a great example of another trigger situation. It's a non-stop, 24-hour-food-bonanza, culminating in the most extreme trigger situation imaginable. Other trigger situations are picnics where food is all laid out; buffet breakfasts or any kind of buffet at all. All restaurant experiences can pose a problem. You may want to steer clear of potluck situations where food is out, and *unguarded*. When you show up to these events, you know you can get anything you want at any time, and no one will even notice. Danger, danger, danger! Mentally put up the orange cones and crime tape!

You have to make a plan, and now I have one. I do my best to pick a restaurant where they have a calorie count on the menu, or I'll even read the menu in advance and have in mind what I'm going to order. When I get to the restaurant, I order a plain salad with no dressing, so I have something to chew on right away. I grab some water with no ice, chug that down. If I know I'm going to be in a situation that's a little risky, I might even eat protein before I leave the house, so I don't feel hungry when I hit the restaurant. There are about 120 calories in four ounces of protein. Look at it from this perspective: if it saves you from the thousands of calories that are waiting for you on the menu, so much the better!

Keep in mind; the food is not going to be as clean as what you cook yourself at home. Even if you ask for the protein to be poached, steamed, baked, or broiled with nothing on it, you never know how it's cooked. Maybe they injected some fat into the meat to make it more tender. Even though you can never quite know, you can have forethought, and say to yourself: *okay this is how I'm going to manage this. I'm going to look for the salad bar, and I'm going to pick the low-calorie items only like lettuce, cucumbers, and peppers. I'm going to stay away from the croutons, the cheese, and other high-calorie items. I'm going to put the salad dressing on the side, and maybe dip my fork in it.*

I don't want to be tempted, so I don't have them bring anything on the side anymore. I don't even want to see those yummy, delicious sauces. I usually ask for lemons and limes for fish, and even for chicken. If you're eating meat, try to keep it as clean as possible. Usually, I substitute the carbohydrate side for double vegetable sides, although some carbohydrates are okay. It's hard when you're in a restaurant to make sure they're clean. That's the challenge that we need to remember. Baked potatoes usually come slathered, but you can have a small portion of a clean potato, or sweet potato, instead of fries. The basic rule is that if you're eating more carbohydrates, you should keep your fats low. You don't want your fats and carbohydrates both to be high. As I mentioned before, fats and carbs are two major energy sources. The trick is to keep one low if the other one is high. Otherwise, the extra energy and calories will be stored as fat.

Converting Triggers Into Supporters

The best thing you can do with a trigger person is to ask for their help and to communicate with them. If you're feeling like you're going to have issues with not being able to control your consumption of certain foods at a restaurant, ask them if they can order something that you won't have a challenge with like vegetables or rice. If they order rice, you won't be as likely to pick the rice off their plate as you would if they had ordered fries. Negotiating at the restaurant probably isn't the best time for the discussion either, so make sure to have that conversation in advance.

It is more important to deal various triggers early in your fitness and health journey. As you become increasingly comfortable with the process of sticking with healthy foods, it will get easier to deal with the trigger foods, people, and situations. Then again, if they're addiction foods, this may not be the case, and you may need reinforcements and some counseling. People can be addicted to food just like alcoholics are addicted to alcohol. People who are true alcoholics can't touch alcohol. I'm a no-alcohol person because calories add up fast. Certain people with certain food addictions can't touch the foods that they're addicted to. In the beginning, you may not be clear on your trigger foods. It's better to avoid them, and have your loved ones avoid them, too—as best as they can. My husband keeps a stash he hides from me now. I don't want to know where it is because I might be too tempted to raid it, but sometimes I ask for a little tidbit from his stash. Now, we can joke about it. At least, most days we can.

Asking for help from friends and loved ones is essential to getting the support you need to achieve your goals. You don't know if you can turn them into your cheerleaders until you try to work with them and have the conversations that will help them to understand the importance of what you have undertaken. Don't write them off. Remember, they love you and probably want you to succeed in achieving your health and fitness goals.

CHAPTER 16

Combatting Depression

DEPRESSION AFFECTS BOTH GENDERS. However, women are more likely than men to be diagnosed. The explanation for this is not fully understood, but it is important to understand depression is not normal, and it is also not a sign of weakness. Unfortunately, many people suffering from depression do NOT seek treatment and suffer in silence.

It is unnecessary to live with this type of pain and struggle because there are effective treatments, even for severe depression. The most important point to remember is that people do not have to suffer needlessly.

Symptoms

People with depression may have a variety of symptoms, and these symptoms will vary from person to person. It is possible some people may have one or two symptoms while others may have many symptoms. The length of time people suffer with symptoms and how often they experience symptoms may even vary.

According to Womenshealth.gov, symptoms of depression include:

- Feeling sad, anxious, "empty" or hopeless

- Loss of interest in activities (including hobbies) that were once enjoyed

- Decreased energy

- Difficulty staying focused, remembering, making decisions

- Sleeplessness, early morning awakening, oversleeping and not wanting to get up

- No desire to eat, weight loss OR eating to "feel better" and weight gain

- Thoughts of hurting oneself, death or suicide (especially worrisome if they have a plan)

- Easily annoyed, bothered, or angered

- Frequent physical symptoms that do not get better with treatment, such as headaches, frequent stomachaches, and pain that does NOT resolve

Screening For Depression

Screening for major depression involves identifying the presence of at least five of the following symptoms (the acronym for these five symptoms is referred to as "SIGE CAPS," and the symptoms must be present for at least two weeks):

- Sleep - increased or decreased (if decreased, then often early morning awakening, too)

- Interest - decreased

- Guilt or worthlessness

- Energy - decreased or fatigue

- Concentration - difficulty making decisions

- Appetite and/or weight increase or decrease

- Psychomotor (movement tied to conscious mental processes) activity - increased or decreased

If you think you might be depressed, please urgently seek help from a qualified mental health professional such as a therapist, social worker, psychiatrist or even a nurse practitioner with mental health expertise. You may also go to your primary care provider, an urgent care center, or an emergency room. If you are feeling suicidal, or homicidal, please call 911 immediately.

CHAPTER 17

Maintaining Weight Loss Over Time

WE KNOW LOSING WEIGHT is challenging. However, keeping weight off and not regaining it is even more challenging. Literature supports that most people gain back the weight they lose and then some, meaning they often gain even more weight back than they originally lost.

There is very little encouraging research to support the successful maintenance of weight loss over time. That does not mean it is impossible. However, specific measures must be taken to increase the likelihood of maintaining weight loss over the long haul. Conscience, diligent, consistent effort is required in addition to employing specific strategies.

Remember, planning is critically important. Plan ahead for what you will eat at work, for what you will eat at night when you come home from work tired and more likely to slip and review restaurant menus before you go out to eat. When you travel, what healthy foods can you pack and carry on the plane? Consistency is key, and planning helps maintain that consistency. Remember, the adage I fall back on: "Fail to prepare. Prepare to fail."

Consistency in your healthy eating choices and also in your exercise program is key. Lack of consistency can lead to regaining weight and losing momentum and motivation. If the wheels start falling off your transformation wagon, get back on track as soon as possible. Get help, recommit and think of all the reasons you want to maintain your awesome transformation. Place these reasons on sticky notes and post them in your house or even create a virtual message, on a screensaver or in your notes app in your phone. Maybe use a powerful reminder like a before and after photo, and place it in a location where you will see it frequently.

Other strategies include exercising about 60-90 minutes (may be split up during the day), most days of the week. Another strategy is to add weightlifting/resistance training to your exercise program.

Unfortunately, we begin to lose muscle (and bone) at age thirty. One benefit of building muscle through weightlifting is that it increases our metabolism allowing us to burn more calories! How great is that? Weightlifting can help people lose weight, but it can also help people keep the weight off. What a neat tip! Weightlifting and resistance training also increase muscle and bone mass, so you get extra benefits over time when you perform this type of exercise.

Another strategy is to keep a food diary. Research has found that food diaries help people self-monitor their food intake (both type and quantity.) People who use food diaries tend to be more successful in reaching their weight loss goals. I know this has been my experience over the last three years. In fact, if I have to write down all my nibbles, licks and bits of goodies I am far less likely to eat them.

When you are shooting for long-term transformation, it's imperative to maintain a network of supportive friends and a supportive environment. The two go hand in hand. Surround yourself with people who eat healthy and live healthy lives. If you have friends you go out to eat with who also generally make healthy choices; it is a lot easier for you to make healthy choices, too. It is a positive influence when others in your environment are like-minded in their decisions and life preferences. In sharp contrast, if you go out to dinner with people eating tempting, unhealthy foods and you are trying to eat healthy, it is much more challenging. Peer influence can be both positive and negative.

You might find maintaining a system of accountability is an effective tactic to employ as well. An example of this would be if you were to go to regular Weight Watchers meetings, or meet with the trainer at your gym on a regular basis or work out with friends, or check in with healthy friends or maybe start or join a Facebook group of other like-minded people who are on the same extended plan as you. Using an app and monitoring your weight can also provide accountability and I know this works because I have been regularly monitoring my weight for three years and the feedback I get from this keeps me on track. When you combine these strategies, you have an even better chance of succeeding!

Building your awareness should be one of your primary goals. Remind yourself that the odds are against you. There is not much encouraging research to support that people can maintain their weight loss over time—BUT IT CAN BE DONE! Are you totally committed to maintaining your transformation? If not, why not? What must you do to shift your attitude to a mindset of self-respect and total commitment to yourself? Do you value yourself? If not, why not? Take some time to think about these considerations because if you don't feel worthy, if you don't cherish yourself, you will not be successful over time. MINDSET is a huge piece of this puzzle. What you look like physically including your weight is very much linked to your attitude, thoughts, and beliefs.

If you feel you need some help, consider either a life coach or therapist/counselor. Several of my favorite life coaches are listed in the resources section, and you can also locate a coach through the coaching federation. In addition, you can ask your primary care provider (NP, PA, midwife or physician) for a referral to a therapist.

And finally, other habits that are often "make or break" concepts are to eat healthy foods you like and participate in exercise that you enjoy. You are more likely to maintain a program both short and long-term if you feel positively about it. This is probably a major reason why people fall off the wagon. People do not like the food they are required to eat in so many diets, nor do they enjoy the activity programs recommended for them. Instead of gaining joy from their positive decisions, they count down the days, hours and minutes until they can go back to their old ways. If instead, people would just eat the healthy foods they like, then they would be far more likely to stick with their program for the duration they need and to make the lasting changes they desire.

CHAPTER 18

Extreme Stress Requires Extreme Self-Care

WHEN OUR STRESS LEVELS go up, that's when we need to take action, and take care of ourselves to counteract the stress effects. Extreme stress requires extreme self-care, but I realize this seems counterintuitive—unless we practice and create a new habit.

What you might notice instead, as one of the first symptoms of extreme stress, is that you've lost pleasure in your life.

Eventually, you will start skipping your workouts, and one day leads to another day, which leads to another day until you notice you're not using that gym membership you're paying for every month. **Maybe you're saying to yourself,** *I'd use it, but I have no time. I have these obligations, and I have to meet them. Exercise and eating healthy doesn't fit in.*

Loss of joy in your life, the loss of a sense of humor, the loss of wanting connection with friends and stopping the things that would normally give you joy are all signs that you're heading toward burnout—if you aren't already there. You might even be depressed. If you are not sure, see your healthcare professional or a therapist, as I've previously mentioned.

It doesn't have to be that way. **Let me share with you the steps that you can take for extreme self-care. Practicing extreme self-care involves meeting your own needs no matter what.**

An example of extreme self-care is bringing a healthy lunch to work with you. It doesn't have to be a three-course meal. Even if it's something as minimal as protein powder, it's still beneficial and better than skipping meals. If you're on the type of schedule that keeps you too busy to eat all day, you can mix the protein powder with some water and drink it quickly to get nutrients into your body. That's extreme and a great example of self-care because the worst thing you can do is go all day without eating. As I have mentioned, when you skip meals it slows your metabolism and contributes to weight gain. It's also hard to think when you are not eating well throughout your workday. Remember to start your day with high protein and complex carbs with a large glass of water, since this will jump-start your metabolism, and help mental clarity and performance.

Extreme self-care may also involve taking a couple of minutes to do some deep breathing, what we call "paced respirations," where you mentally take yourself to the beach or maybe the mountains for a few minutes and think about your sensory experience. Or maybe you envision three words. My favorites are *Peace, Love, Joy*. I close my eyes and breathe in slowly to the count of three, and exhale to the count of five. I repeat this for a couple of minutes. Maybe all you have *is* a couple of minutes. That's another example of extreme self-care in the context of extreme stress. Everyone has one or two minutes. If you're at work and that's all the time you have, this self-care measure will help lower your blood pressure, lower your heart rate, lower your cortisol levels, and bring some joy and peace into your life.

You may not have the time to spend 60 minutes at the gym, an hour with friends or an hour reading a book for pleasure. But you have two minutes to do jumping jacks, jump rope or hula hoop. You can do one heck of a workout even within that timeframe. You can also Google *The New York Times* "Seven-Minute Workout." I guarantee doing that program will get your blood pumping. Likewise, five minutes of bathtub rest can be extremely joyful. Don't forget to light a candle. Just find ways of stopping the continuous stress, no matter what, that's the goal of practicing extreme self-care. Make it a game to find as many two-minute opportunities as possible to improve your mental health. You are worth it.

Wouldn't it be great if we all possessed this extreme self-care skill set so we could plug these skills into the most stressful situations of our lives, rather than crashing-and-burning? This cycle of stress and burnout perpetuates the yo-yo cycle of weight gaining patterns.

Wouldn't it be great if we could be the role models in managing stress, the masters of extreme self-care? Why can't we be?

Before my transformation, I would take care of myself *if* I had extra time, which was rare. Therefore, I did not take good care of myself. Now, I find the time. I plan for self-care activities, and I covet that time by making it happen, no matter what. Again, it comes down to being fully committed to yourself and your goals and feeling worthy—which is contingent on having a positive mindset about yourself.

What I tell people, and women especially, is that it's worth learning these skills because isn't it a wonderful way to live your life when you're full of joy, and when you feel healthy and fit? Think about the last time you went on a vacation with your family, and it was a wonderful vacation. Or imagine some other time when you were very happy. Wouldn't it be great to get to live your life that way all the time?

I believe with all my heart that this goal is possible for each and every one of you reading this book.

I notice how uplifting it is to be around people who are upbeat—we all do. Imagine bringing that authentic joy into your life at work, home and out in the world!

The power we have in the work environment when we're authentically healthy, happy and fit is so much more positively impactful than when we go to work, and we're resentful, anxious, stressed out, and exhausted, period.

We can't afford *not* to meet our own needs. We cannot serve from an empty vessel. Self-care is not selfish. Self-care is essential to serve others better.

CHAPTER 19

How To Cope With Hyperfocusing

HYPERFOCUSING MEANS YOU CAN'T get something out of your head. You might have in your head that you want ice cream or fries, and it will dominate your every thought. You have it in your head that in the second kitchen cabinet on the right is the perfect donut just waiting for you.

If you can't get these thoughts out of your head, you're at great risk of eating those treats. These cravings may never fully go away, but fighting them can become easier with specific coping strategies.

The number one strategy for combatting hyperfocusing is to minimize the temptation. If you're visual, get them out of your environment. Don't allow the food to be visually apparent. I love Ghirardelli dark chocolate chips, and I would enjoy a handful on occasion. I'd even count them out. I knew exactly how many were in a serving. Then I'd portion out another handful. And then another handful... and another handful. Eventually, I had to give them up. Put them out of sight. Even now I have to be extremely careful. I prefer for them to not even be in my vicinity because they're not an option for me.

The second way of coping is to distract yourself. Keep in your mind what it is you *can* eat instead. Switch from hyperfocusing on the forbidden food to enjoying the pleasure of the food you can eat. Personally, I'm a chomper, and I need things I can crunch on. Can you bite into celery if you desire something crunchy? Can you drink three glasses of water if your stomach feels empty? What is your lineup of food you can munch on if you need to chomp something? The show coach I hired to help me get ready for my show would often remind me early on in my process of what he would do when presented with the same obstacles. As he explained, "I know it's not an option when I'm in prep mode, so I go on to other things. I don't let it pester me." Especially, in the beginning, this may be easier said than done. But, persist anyway. **Remember, everything is hard until it's easy.** Learning how NOT to hyperfocus will become easier.

I realized there was something to that, and eventually, it clicked. We have control over our minds, and that's all we have control over. You have to play a game of sorts with your mind to switch over to focusing on the foods you can eat, and the joyful pleasure that it will give you. It works most of the time. Nothing works all the time. That's what makes this process so challenging. But eventually, our minds will begin to work with us, and if we keep at it the healthy foods we had to force ourselves to focus on at one time become foods we look forward to.

In the beginning, I thought eating chicken every three hours was going to be so boring. Now I look forward to it. I so look forward to egg whites! I like them early in the morning, and I like them late at night. They've taken the place of my ice cream bedtime snack. I have egg whites with cinnamon. That's the equivalent of a bowl of ice cream for me, and I love it. Changing to egg whites from ice cream was an acquired preference that took time and practice to develop.

Did I always love egg whites and chicken? No way! I was so mad when I could no longer have ice cream every day. This was my resistance to change rearing its ugly head. Now, I know it is not serving me to eat that bowl of ice cream unless it happens to be part of a weekly treat meal. This is the benefit of scheduling the occasional treat meal for yourself because you can get that craving out of your system. That is, as long as it's not an addiction. (See THE WEEKLY "TREAT" MEAL in Chapter 2). It's priceless to be able to indulge periodically and can give you something to look forward to. If you let it, it can sustain you from week-to-week. Having a treat meal once a week does that for me. Remember, it may boost your metabolism too, as it helps with your weight loss.

CHAPTER 20

"Sundowning" And Losing Willpower

S
UNDOWNING IS A TERM borrowed from elder care to describe behaviors such as mental confusion that tends to occur later in the day, especially in the early evening. When I use this term in the context of achieving a healthy lifestyle, I'm referring to the tendency to lose our willpower when we are tired and worn out. This can lead us to overeat and be tempted to indulge in other ways.

Our willpower naturally declines over the day as our bodies and minds get worn out and tired. We tend to have less ability to resist temptation at the end of the day. This affects some people more than others, so you have to take your pulse on this. Do you sundown? If so, to what extent? What happens when you sundown? Are you at risk of losing the wheels off your wagon and veering into the gutter—by indulging in your favorite treats and goodies? How must you rearrange your life so you can cope with your sundowning tendencies and specific situations that arise when you have less willpower?

Again, for me, it comes back to the quote, "Fail to prepare. Prepare to fail." You don't want to head into your evenings after a busy day at work having to confront and combat all sorts of temptations. You want to come home to healthy food options. You want to come home to a situation where you feel like you are in control.

Prepare for that visceral reaction. What do you need to do for yourself so when you do come home from work, the house is a safe place, the home environment has been prepared properly, so you'll be okay? Do you prep your food earlier in the day? Do you have to hide certain foods from yourself, or give them to a family member to stow somewhere? Maybe you stop buying certain foods, so they are not in your environment. I can keep forbidden foods in my garage, but if they find their way into the kitchen, I'm in trouble especially at night when I sundown.

I try to food prep as early in the day as possible when my mind and body are rested. I find food prepping while preparing dinner is also a good time, as I am in the kitchen anyway, watching the news or listening to it. I know I don't want to wait until later in the evening when I'm vegetative and sundowning. That's a recipe for disaster! You might find food prepping on weekends works well for you, and then you can be on semi-automatic during your busy work week. You can even arrange your food into meal-size portions, so they are grab-and-go ready.

When it comes to food prep, there is major and minor food prep. Major food prep is when you're cooking up a big batch of protein, cutting it and measuring it into portions— whether it's baggies, or plastic containers, or whatever you want to use—and then stuffing it all into your freezer. That's what we call major food prep, and it can take a lot of time. At the very least, a few hours.

Minor food prep, then, is getting yourself ready for the next day. I set up my breakfast the night before, and I'll prepare what I imagine I'll need to take with me to have throughout the day. This is especially important if I'm going to be away from home while at work, or out for appointments and shopping. I may even organize some of the things I'll need for dinner that night or the next day. If it's a day I'll be at home, I want to plan in my mind what I'm going to eat every three hours for most of the day, and I may physically organize it as well. Then you're not trying to deal with it when you're hungry. When we're hungry, that's when we're most vulnerable, and we're *all* at risk of making unhealthy choices under those circumstances. After all, we are human.

If we can get help dealing with these potential moments, that can be key because it eases anxiety and stress levels by allowing you to shift your focus to other tasks that need to be addressed. Getting help is essential in easing our burdens and increasing our chances of success. This is especially important in the evening when we are tired and often the most vulnerable to temptations.

If making time isn't an option, you could use your crockpot earlier in the day, or over the weekend, so you have a meal ready. Then all you have to do is warm it up. I think we need to be far more proactive in our own lives. Food prep allows you to increase your proactivity.

We have to work around our temperaments, and our tendencies, and we have to be aware that our brains will wear out at the end of the day.

So, goes our willpower as well. Failing to prepare is a recipe for disaster and self-sabotage.

And then what?

You are then at risk of crashing and burning, so to speak, as manifested by giving into your whims, whatever they may be. It could be junk food, alcohol, skipping exercise, staying up too late, watching too much TV, etc.

Section V:
ENVIRONMENT

CHAPTER 21

Finding The Right Team

ASSEMBLING THE RIGHT TEAM for your needs involves doing your homework and being proactive.

Sometimes, this can involve some trial and error. I had a trainer early on in the process who was younger, and he didn't have as much knowledge about how to deal with older female clients who'd had injuries they must work around. I always had aches and pains, and never felt like I was in the groove with this trainer. You must listen to your inner voice. If you are not feeling comfortable with a trainer, then it might be time to move on.

So, I looked around, and found someone who could help me learn to lift weights properly, a trainer who worked with older clients, and with people who have had past injuries or have current limitations. It was a perfect fit. She was my go-to resource when I was having pain doing certain exercises on my own. She'd always teach me another way to work that muscle group without causing an aggravation of whatever-the-problem-was. She was usually able to analyze the problem and figure out what I was doing wrong.

To find good trainers, it helps to ask someone at your gym, or in your community. Physical therapists may have their finger on the pulse of good trainers as well. In a lot of gyms, you can watch trainers while you're doing cardio, and that can be a smart way to vet a prospective trainer. I have two trainers I work with now at my gym—you can never have enough good trainers—and I watched both of them work with clients. When I hired them, I knew they were both competent. When you are first starting out, you might not have enough experience or knowledge to evaluate trainers. So, this is why you want to ask others, especially physical therapists. You might also interview trainers and their clients. Introduce yourself and start a discussion, preferably when they are not working out with a client. If this pertains to you, ask the trainer if they work with "older" clients and if they also work with folks who have limitations or aches/pains.

It's always a smart idea to interview people and try them out, too. It is important to give them a trial period. There needs to be a match in energy, personality, and expertise they can offer you. It's like shopping for a car, but I think even more important. If it's not the right match, it's time to move on and find someone else. You must have a good communication system with your trainer; to ensure they hear what your concerns are, and can address them effectively. If you feel like they're not getting you, it could be a mismatch, leading to potential problems down the road. If you think you're not progressing, if you're having lots of aches and pains during and after your workout, that's never good. It might be time to check out another trainer who will better suit you.

CHAPTER 22

Creating A Supportive Environment

EXTERNAL FORCES IN YOUR environment, like friends, family, lack of their support and physical circumstances, can make or break our success by impacting our ability to reach our goals. They can make it easier or much more difficult. I know this because I live it every day.

You do, too.

According to the CDC, determinants of health include social support.

Having supportive friends, family and coworkers can make a world of difference. If support is so crucial to our success, then why do so many people go it alone when it comes to changing their lives or pursuing their dreams and goals? That is the million-dollar question.

Learning how to create a supportive environment and how to manipulate your environment, are essential skills required to achieve and maintain a successful life transformation.

It is essential to continue to hone our skills because we all will be continuously challenged by our environment—new people, new places, new circumstances, new enticing foods—that will test our commitment and skills.

This section will provide you with the knowledge and skills you need to cope with a variety of environmental challenges successfully. These are my tried and true tips and tricks I use every day, and I can tell you from personal experience they are very effective.

Perhaps from having numerous conversations with women and men over the years about this topic, I've noticed it is a conundrum for most people. This is because most people know what they should do, and will tell me that and then they will go on to say, "I just have to do it." If it were that simple, everyone would be living their dream life and look like their dream self. Unfortunately, it is far more complicated.

In our home environment, we may have significant others who also have weight issues or other health challenges, or we may live with people who don't worry or don't think they have to worry. We may have loved ones who are supportive of our health and fitness goals, or we may have loved ones who are not supportive, or who are neutral and don't really care. Depending on who you're surrounded by, you may need to dig deep into your own motivation, and not let external forces in the home environment (or any environment for that matter), derail you from your success. Instead, **you want to set up your home environment to ensure you succeed.** It can be done.

Many of you may have children, and children have special nutritional needs, but their main need is to eat healthy. They must eat a balanced, healthy diet, just as you should. Rather than having junk food around, replace it with healthy food alternatives for you, your family and your housemates. Replace the junk food with some healthy snacks; chop up some vegetables, so healthy options are readily available. This way when individuals around the house are hungry, they can grab for food that's ready to go, that's not processed, and not junk food. When protein is cooked and in measured portions, you can grab what is needed, and it is very convenient.

Get the unhealthy food out of the cabinets; maybe even lock it away if you've got someone who doesn't care what they eat, or who can eat anything they want. Maybe you literally need to purchase a locked cabinet so they can put their stuff in there, and only they know the combination. If a problem is easy access to foods you are choosing to avoid, creative measures may be necessary. You might think a locked cabinet is an extreme measure, but I would suggest it is not if this will keep you on track with your goals. You may find over time, as I did, that having tempting foods in your environment becomes easier, but sometimes that is not the case. Especially with trigger foods or those we are addicted to. So, cut yourself some slack and do what you must to stay on track! Remember, if you are fully committed, you will do what it takes, no matter what.

Even when traveling, I have to junk-food-proof my hotel room. When I go to a hotel, and they have the minibar unlocked, I'll ask them to take the minibar out. I don't want access to it. If it's visually out there, that's even worse. I'm sure they think to themselves, *we've got a weirdo here*, but if this is what I need to do to ensure I stay on track, it's worth it. Sometimes I get gifts like complimentary baskets that I receive as a thank you for speaking at an event. These can be a problem. Inside, I might find crackers and cheese, candies, and goodies. These foods can be very tempting. I have to explain to the hotel staff, "I'm sorry, but there's nothing here I can eat. You can give it to somebody else. Knock on the door next to me, and surprise them." Do what is necessary, no matter what it is, to stay the course on your health journey in order to achieve your goals. You can do it.

In the beginning, my approach was much more extreme. I would say, "Get all this food out of here! I can't have crackers. I can't have bread. I can't have dinner rolls, or ice cream, or cheese, or even cottage cheese. I can't have any of that in the house right now." I'm sure it was really traumatic for my husband because the options I gave him were either don't buy it or put it somewhere else where I can't

162

see it. Donuts, muffins, chocolate, ice cream, chips, all the goodies that we'd normally have in the house, that we had enjoyed together, all off-limits. Tasty bits, candy...it had to go somewhere else. Man, was I "moving his cheese." Until recently, I did not realize how much of an impact that probably had on him.

Only recently, two-and-a-half-years later, am I able to live in the midst of some of that forbidden junk food. Even so, I'm apprehensive about gaining weight. So, I'm very cautious when I test the waters in terms of what I can get away with while still maintaining my weight in post-show mode. It's an ongoing challenge, as I think it is for most people. That's why we don't have much research on patients successfully keeping their weight off. In addition to the fact that I personally think a lot of folks want to be over the process of being deprived. Too many people see dieting as a finite project, and once they have reached their goal, they can go back to the way they were and the lifestyle they enjoyed previously. For most of us, that's completely flawed thinking. Indeed, it is the harsh reality that most of us are facing: a lifetime of challenge to keep our weight within a reasonable range to maintain our health.

Now, I'm hoping that as I build more muscle, my metabolism will rev up so I can consume more calories without gaining weight. But I'm not sure yet because I have a turtle's metabolism. It takes mountains to move my metabolism. It's always been that way. **For anyone to say to me,** *"Oh, it's probably easy for you,"* **I reply: "No, it's not easy for me. I'm no different than anyone else."**

During one six-month period in my early weight loss journey, several years ago, when I was unable to lose weight on 1,200 calories a day, it took a nutritional consultation to figure out why I was "stuck". I added once a week treat meals, added variable cardio (alternating HITT, then LISS [Low Intensity Steady State cardio].) I added more calories, then, "surprise," I started losing weight again. The solution was counterintuitive. The big take home message: If you're plateauing, get an expert consultation with a coach, trainer, nutritionist, dietician, sports medicine expert, or bariatrics specialist. Whatever you do, don't give up.

CHAPTER 23

Limitations Of Working With Loved Ones

MY DAUGHTER AND I have worked really hard on our relationship. But, there are still times when we push each other, and I don't hear what she says. Or, I don't react well to what she tells me, or suggests to me. At times, she'll have the same problem with me. Naturally, there are things I do that pester her, and at certain points she puts her emotional wall up, indicating she needs her space. I call it switching channels. She goes from what I consider to be her normal self, to putting up the wall, and turns me off. That pattern can be very hard on me. I can't help but be hurt by it, but I am learning to speak up, share my feelings and also hear what she has to say, without interrupting and without thinking about what I will say next. True listening is a skill that can be improved. When someone is talking, do you really listen or do you think about what you will say next while that person is talking?

Katherine and I have worked out a system that's remarkable, but we still have limitations and relationship challenges, and we know it. But very recently, we have made progress in this pattern, and I am so grateful. Working hard on a relationship is super challenging, but the breakthroughs are well worth the blood, sweat, and tears.

I often tell people Katherine was a spirited child. This is a nice way of saying she is wild as the wind. My labor was very challenging and culminated in an emergency C-Section because of complications. Fortunately, we were both OK and came home after a few days in the hospital.

I have to share this funny story. I meditated an hour every day in my pregnancy in an effort to have a calm "Buddha" baby. That is a baby with a serene nature. Well, so much for that plan. However, I am very glad I meditated in pregnancy and continue to practice meditation as part of my self-care habits.

This was just the beginning of quite an experience parenting this spirited child. She started out with severe colic, and the only way to console her was to either bounce her vertically (not side-to-side or in a wind-up swing—she didn't like either) or to place her on the clothes dryer (my husband and I created a changing table with a strap) so we could set her down for 10 minutes. The vibration of the dryer would calm her down. We had listened to a radio program about colic, and they suggested building a secure changing table on the clothes dryer and setting the timer to create a vibration that would likely soothe the crankiest baby. AND IT WORKED.

It was very fortunate that she was adorable because she continued to be a challenge through every developmental phase. Always curious, endless energy, up early every morning and late to go to bed despite a bedtime routine and lots of storytelling. She was charming but also stubborn and could fly into a rage without warning. She did not transition easily, and that made parenting her very stressful.

Now, I realize that her uniquely spirited, energetic, and creative personality are huge assets. This is especially apparent to me as we work together to help others become healthy, confident and successful in their lives.

I've realized the more closely we work together, the harder it can be at times because people get on your nerves when they're loved ones. I don't understand it. I don't like it, but I know it to be true. You've got to have your own space, and you've got to accept and respect that in others, as well. Sometimes, learning how to exercise and eat healthy are not good endeavors to take on with our loved ones...no matter how much we might want that to be the case. Remember, you are your own top priority.

Katherine and I worked out together off-and-on for more than two years when I was first starting my health/

fitness journey. That's a long period of time, and I didn't realize how frustrating it was to Katherine, who's an accomplished weightlifter and athlete. I didn't realize how much working with me caused her to interrupt her own workouts. She really doesn't get the quality of workout with me that she would otherwise get working out on her own or with another comparable athlete.

Katherine and I finally had to have what she refers to as a "gym divorce." We do our own workouts now, except for once in a while, but the way I look at it is that she has cut me free. She needs to meet her own needs, and I need to meet my own needs. I always felt inept when I worked out with her. And I was worried I'd be at risk of injuring myself because I'd push myself so much when I worked out with her that I did actually hurt myself several times. That wasn't good for either of us. She worried about me, and I worried about myself.

I got under her skin, especially because even though I am a nurse practitioner, I didn't always understand what exercises worked what muscles. This went on for a long time. It is not intuitive. You must learn, and someone must teach you.

It is important to give ourselves time to learn the correct technique to lift weights. It isn't necessarily intuitive to understand what muscles we're working out when we do different exercises. It takes learning and practice. Some might grasp it sooner than others, and that is perfectly okay.

That's why it's great to hire, and pay for, a trainer. If you think that a trainer costs too much money—well, I will tell you it's the best money you're going to spend. To have someone teach you how to perform exercises properly is the key to demystifying the gym. There's nothing more intimidating than walking into the gym as a female, especially a postmenopausal female, and looking at all the people you think are competently lifting weights while you're trying to figure out how to fit in. It's overwhelming. That's why a lot of women, especially women of my demographic, will walk into the gym, and find where the cardio room is and where the classes are located. Sound familiar? That's what we do. There are very few women over 40 who are comfortable walking into the weightlifting area of the gym to start lifting weights.

Even if you hire a trainer only once a month, it helps to meet with someone regularly to learn the process of what to do, and on which machine or free weights. Incorrect technique can lead to injury. Injury is also more likely to occur as we get older, especially when we are over 40, or have had injuries in the past.

It is also very important to communicate with your trainer about how you are feeling. If you have pain, tell the trainer. If you have soreness after a workout, tell your trainer. If you have specific pain somewhere, be sure to tell your trainer, and they will figure out a way to adapt your exercise program. "No pain, no gain" is an adage that has very little place in workout programs today.

You can also minimize injury by being well-hydrated, following a healthy protein-focused eating plan, and getting adequate sleep.

CHAPTER 24

Staying Healthy On The Go

THE SECRET TO STAYING healthy while traveling is all about preparation and having a game plan. If you fail to prepare you better prepare to fail in the context of traveling because it challenges even savvy, experienced travelers like me.

When you're traveling, whether it's for a vacation or a business trip, you need to make a plan for maintaining your health. While you're packing your clothes, you also need to think about what you're going to do about food. Are there some snacks, or protein bars, you can pack in your luggage? Can you find protein powder in single-serving packets you can stash or pack in your carry-on? Maybe some tuna foil packs, or some other ready-made food that you can bring with you, so you're more prepared? Can you buy or prepare little baggies of portioned-out nuts? Getting ready for a trip includes preparing for the food challenges you're going to face while you travel.

You must avoid hunger that results from not being prepared. Otherwise, you will be tempted to indulge—especially when traveling. I think Aunt Annie's Pretzels pumps the aroma of their pretzels out into the air we breathe at airports to tempt us. It's like the Pied Piper, and it works. So, you better fend them off by making healthy food choices consistently when you travel. DO NOT let yourself get ravenously hungry, especially when you are in an airport.

I usually bring a serving of chicken or other lean protein, at least one serving that I can have when I get to the airport. Then I'm not hitting the airport hungry, tempted to give in to all the treats that can be found in close range. I try to never get on an airplane without healthy food, and a container of water. You never know when you're going to be sitting on the tarmac for hours. Remember, drinking extra water while traveling is good for you and it helps with jet lag as it prevents dehydration and assists you in coping with the stresses of travel.

Even if I have food packed in my computer bag for emergencies, I prefer fresh food when I am at an airport. I will often go on a hunt to find a healthy and fairly fresh salad. I have this "hunt" down to an art form! Sometimes, I even video this process and post it online. I'll go by one kiosk after another, after another, until I see a salad that looks halfway decent. There's nothing worse than opening a salad with brown, slimy lettuce. Often, I'll get on an airplane with a salad that I've purchased elsewhere, because I much prefer real food over no food or junk food, that are often your only options on airplanes.

I have a unique situation in that I travel so much I can get upgraded to first-class quite frequently, which you would think would be a perk I love. But it can be hard for someone like me who is either working to get leaner or to maintain my current state of fitness, because what do they do when you sit down in your seat? They ask you if you want a drink, if you want alcohol, if you want a little goodie, if you want cookies or anything in the tray that they bring by a thousand times in a two-hour flight. I had to stop eating all those goodies when I began this fitness transformation because it wasn't working for me. Their meals don't tend to be healthy either, so I don't find much value in the upgrade, other than the bigger seats and a little extra TLC from the flight attendants. Getting an upgrade is not a perk you look forward to if you're working on losing weight or maintaining your weight.

Exercise while traveling can also be challenging because when you're traveling, you're often exhausted. Sometimes the travel day is grueling, especially if you've awakened early and arrived late to your destination. I do walk whenever I can in the airports. Walking between connection times is a great way to fit cardio into your day, and get your blood flowing again after being cooped up on the airplane for hours.

For me, too late to go to the gym is 10 o'clock at night. I prefer to start my workout before nine, but any workout is better than no workout! I will do both my cardio and weightlifting as long as I can get to the gym before 10 o'clock...even if I have to drag myself in there. I've made a personal rule now that if I want to watch TV, it'd better be in the gym. It's not going to happen in my room, because what happens when you turn on the TV in your room? Usually, you lie down on the bed, and for me, that's a death blow. If I lie down on the bed, I'm in trouble because I probably will not want to get out of that bed after traveling all day. The rare exception is if I get in early enough, I might set my alarm for a short nap, and then force myself out of bed and into the gym. I rarely skip a day. I try to do something every single day. The hardest part is getting your body out of bed and then standing up. If I can do it, so can you! It's a habit you can learn!

I used to succumb. **I used to think I was too tired to exercise, too tired to eat healthy, and that was my mantra. I now recognize those were all excuses.** I'm older now; it should be harder for me. But it's actually easier for me today because I've practiced and have developed discipline and healthy habits. I'm using my mindset to my advantage. I talk to myself and say, *you can do it. You can do it. You know you can do it; get yourself out of the hotel room to the gym, and you'll be doing it.* Sometimes I place my sneakers on my bed next to me (on a towel, of course) when I nap, so as soon as the alarm goes off, I can put my shoes on. My other mantra is *No Excuses*.

I used to think it wasn't healthy to exercise after eating, and I do that all the time now while traveling. I'll eat a light meal, frequently with business colleagues, and then I'll go exercise afterward, as long as it's before 10 o'clock. I can go to bed immediately after exercise on most nights. In fact, it often puts me to sleep. I've read that exercising before you go to sleep isn't a good idea because you will be too stimulated to sleep, but that's a mindset. It doesn't have to be that way. You can adapt any process or schedule you like as long as it works and moves you closer to achieving your goals. Remember, *No Excuses* is my mantra. Perhaps you will consider adopting my mantra, too?

CONCLUSION

Your Transformation With Coach Kat And Dr. Mimi

I F YOU STILL HAVE dreams you want to pursue, and you are still breathing—it's never too late. You are never too old to make a big change in your health and life because age is just a number.

Together, we have explored how to optimize your nutrition, exercise, mindset, environment, and team. Even if you are stressed out, tired and time-scarce. So, by this stage, I hope you realize that transforming your health and life is *much more than just making changes in exercise and nutrition.* They are just one part of the equation. To truly transform your life, you must integrate all aspects of your mind, body, and spirit, to ensure the changes last.

Of course, reading this book and knowing what to do isn't enough. Because knowledge isn't knowledge until you put it into action. Even if you know what needs to be done, the reality is, *execution* comes with challenges. When you are exploring uncharted territory, you need a coach who has been where you have been. Elite athletes and high-performing business people don't reach their peak alone. They all have a coach or a mentor. You need someone to support you when the going gets tough, someone to identify your blind spots and someone who refuses to let you settle for anything less than your full potential.

As a direct result of working with Katherine and my trainers, preparing and performing my "debut at 62", and transforming my health and life—Katherine and I had our own "aha" moment.

"Look, Katherine, this is really incredible what you did with me. What if it was possible for us to help other women (and men) healthcare professionals like nurse practitioners become healthier, more confident, and more successful?"

The idea of our dynamic mother/daughter duo was born: "Coach Kat and Dr. Mimi."

Kat and I now own and operate our coaching business together: **www.CoachKatandDoctorMimi.com**, empowering nurse practitioners, healthcare professionals, and busy on-the-go women and men with the tools and know-how to transform their health and their lives.

Where to from here? Sign up for your FREE 15-Minute Coaching Call. Visit **www.CoachKatandDoctorMimi.com** to get started now. Together, we will help you clarify what your health/fitness/life goals are and if we are a right fit to continue working with one another. You may walk away clearer about what is important to you, and confident in what next steps to take.

Our coaching programs go beyond just regaining your physical health and appearance. What we offer is an opportunity to *Debut a New You,* empowering all aspects of your life including relationships, personal purpose, career, and health.

Acknowledgments

TO MY BELOVED DAUGHTER, Katherine, AKA Coach Kat, my coach, trainer, mentor, biggest supporter, and the driving force behind my transformation. I know it has not been easy working with your mom. However, I owe my new healthy life to you. I gave birth to you, Katherine, and you poignantly gave birth to me in helping to transform my life. At age 59, if I had not turned my life around the consequences would have been potentially life-threatening and most certainly would have impacted my quality of life. I thank you, Katherine, from the bottom of my heart.

To my mom, Irene, who always encouraged me to take risks and believe in myself, and whose incredible love has sustained me throughout my life.

To my sweet husband, Mike, who supports me no matter what crazy thing I want to do. Without his help and unconditional love, I would not have been able to accomplish my goal to "Debut at 62."

To my travel friends and professional colleagues, Amelie and Jeanie, who encouraged me to "GoMimiGo" when I wasn't in the mood to work out or eat healthy. You have made many sacrifices to help me achieve my goals.

To my life coach of more than 15 years, Morgaine Beck, who helped me clean up my inner house, so I could believe in myself. You have helped me build my confidence and emotional strength so that I could quiet my doubting gremlins and trust my true self. You have made my transformation possible and I am eternally grateful.

To Bonnie Pappas, my first official trainer who taught me how to lift weights, avoid injuries, work around aches and pains, and how to pose for my first bodybuilding show. I am grateful for your guidance.

To my bodybuilding show coach, Bill Anger, who helped me achieve something I never thought would be possible—stepping on stage in a bikini at age 62! Thank you for your wisdom, expertise, support and endless patience as we together figured out how to work with my—at times—stubborn metabolism.

Thanks to my current workout trainers, Diana Piscitelli and Mark Featherstone. You have both pushed me harder than I thought possible!

Thanks to my home gym, Powerhouse in Plymouth, Massachusetts for your support and friendship. Special thanks to the amazing Powerhouse staff including April,

Bianca, Andy, the trainers and instructors; Diana, Mark, Joe, Lynne, Julie, Tracy, Elise, Zack, Grace, and Kim.

Thanks to my fellow gym peeps including; "Bobzilla," Francine, Donna, Emily, Tom, Bob, Cassie, Sarah, EJ, Craig, Max, Niki, Megan, Kylie, Liz, Ken, Mike and so many others who welcomed me despite my age. Each of you help me keep pushing and believing in myself.

Thanks to all my friends, especially my fellow Rocky Mountain University of Health Professions (RMU) students—now Alum—especially Dr. Barb Spencer.

A special thanks to my Facebook community who have supported me throughout my journey! You are all appreciated.

Thanks to my book cover photographer, Pedro Blanco and to my hair and makeup artist, Kim Richards for working your magic.

Special thanks to first writing collaborator, Reneé Novelle. Reneé was the first person to help me tell my story. Her guidance and support was invaluable.

I would also like to thank my publisher Epic Author Publishing, and it's founder Trevor Crane for helping me expand the mission of my book beyond just sharing my story. With his guidance, and the support of my amazing writers, Hilary Lauren Jastram, Diana Castaldini and Jon Low, this book now has become a work that doesn't just inspire the reader, it gives them the ability to create a practical guide to improve their health, increase their confidence and ultimately create success in their life, career and relationships. This book, and the amazing program I created with my daughter Kat Secor (aka Coach Kat), has now become a vehicle to TRANSFORM LIVES, both personally and professionally.

I would like to thank each and every one of you. I could not have achieved my health and fitness goals or written this book without you.

Resources

Dr. Mimi Secor's Website
www.mimisecor.com

Coach Kat and Dr. Mimi
www.CoachKatandDrMimi.com

Morgaine Beck
Life Coach
Morgaine@treehousecoach.com

Eileen O'Grady, PhD, RN, NP
Certified Nurse Practitioner & Wellness Coach
www.eileenogrady.net

Weight Watchers
www.weightwatchers.com
Programs designed to help participants see food as fuel
for a healthy life, finding ways to move more each day,

and developing the skills to unlock your inner strength so you can make healthy choices for life.

Overeaters Anonymous
https://oa.org/
OA is not just about weight loss, weight gain, maintenance, obesity or diets. OA programs offer physical, emotional, and spiritual recovery for those who suffer from compulsive eating.

International Coach Federation
https://coachfederation.org/
The International Coach Federation (ICF) is the leading global organization dedicated to advancing the coaching profession by setting high standards, providing independent certification and building a worldwide network of trained coaching professionals.

American Cancer Society
ACS.org

American Dietitians Association
ada.org/

American Heart Association
AHA.org

American College of Obstetrics and Gynecology
ACOG.org

American Association of Nurse Practitioners
AANP.org

Centers for Disease Control and Prevention
http://cdc.gov/

Nurse Practitioners in Women's Health
NPWH.org

Apps for Phone/Tablet:
Lose It! Weight Loss App
MyFitnessPal
Pact
Diet Hero
Fooducate
iPhone Health App
Google Fit
7-Minute Workout

References

1. "Supplemental Material for Alcohol's Acute Effect on Food Intake Is Mediated by Inhibitory Control Impairments." *Health Psychology*, 2015. doi:10.1037/hea0000320. supp.

2. Norcross, John C. *Psychotherapy relationships that work: evidence-based responsiveness*. New York: Oxford University Press, 2011.

3. Gibbons, R. J., Balady, G. J., Beasley, J. W., Bricker, J. T., Duvernoy, W. F. C., Froelicher, V. F., ... Ryan, A. "ACC/AHA Guidelines for Exercise Testing: A Report of the American College of Cardiology/American Heart Association Task Force on Practice Guidelines (Committee on Exercise Testing)." *Journal of the American College of Cardiology* (1997): 30(1), 260-311 doi: 10.1016/S0735-1097(97)00150-2

4. Norcross, John C., and Dominic J. Vangarelli. "The resolution solution: Longitudinal examination of New Year's change attempts." *Journal of Substance Abuse*1, no. 2 (1988): 127-34. doi:10.1016/s0899-3289(88)80016-6.

5. Kariba, Yvonne. "10 Reasons We Fail to Achieve Our Goals." The Huffington Post. April 27, 2015. Accessed August 17, 2017. http://www.huffingtonpost.com/yvonne-kariba/10-reasons-we-fail-to-ach_b_7152688.html.

6. Schwantes, Marcel. "Science Says 92 Percent of People Don't Achieve Their Goals. Here's How the Other 8 Percent Do." Inc.com. Accessed August 17, 2017. https://www.inc.com/marcel-schwantes/science-says-92-percent-of-people-dont-achieve-goals-heres-how-the-other-8-perce.html.

7. Diamond, Dan. "Just 8% of People Achieve Their New Year's Resolutions. Here's How They Do It." Forbes. January 02,

2013. Accessed August 17, 2017. https://www.forbes.com/sites/dandiamond/2013/01/01/just-8-of-people-achieve-their-new-years-resolutions-heres-how-they-did-it/.

8. "Keeping It Off." Centers for Disease Control and Prevention. May 15, 2015. Accessed August 17, 2017. https://www.cdc.gov/healthyweight/losing_weight/keepingitoff.html.

9. "Division of Nutrition, Physical Activity, and Obesity." Centers for Disease Control and Prevention. August 09, 2017. Accessed August 1, 2017. https://www.cdc.gov/nccdphp/dnpao/index.html.

10. "The National Weight Control Registry." National Weight Control Registry. Accessed August 17, 2017. http://www.nwcr.ws/.

11. "Determinants of Health." Determinants of Health | Healthy People 2020. Accessed August 19, 2017. https://www.healthypeople.gov/2020/about/foundation-health-measures/Determinants-of-Health#social.

12. Franz, Marion J., Jeffrey J. Vanwormer, A. Lauren Crain, Jackie L. Boucher, Trina Histon, William Caplan, Jill D. Bowman, and Nicolas P. Pronk. "Weight-Loss Outcomes: A Systematic Review and Meta-Analysis of Weight-Loss Clinical Trials with a Minimum 1-Year Follow-Up." *Journal of the American Dietetic Association*107, no. 10 (2007): 1755-767. doi:10.1016/j.jada.2007.07.017.

13. Clear, James. "Habit Stacking: How to Build New Habits by Taking Advantage of Old Ones." James Clear. May 26, 2017. Accessed August 19, 2017. http://jamesclear.com/habit-stacking.

14. Clear, James. "How to Build a New Habit: This is Your Strategy Guide for Changing Habits." James Clear. May 26,

2017. Accessed August 19, 2017. http://jamesclear.com/habit-guide.

15. "National Center for Health Statistics." Centers for Disease Control and Prevention. January 20, 2017. Accessed August 17, 2017. https://www.cdc.gov/nchs/fastats/exercise.htm.

16. Carson, Richard David. *Taming your gremlin: a surprisingly simple method for getting out of your own way*. New York: Quill, 2003.

About Dr. Mimi

D R. MIMI SECOR IS a Nurse Practitioner, National Speaker, Consultant, Award Winning Author and Entrepreneur from Onset, Massachusetts, the gateway to Cape Cod. With over 40 years of experience, she specializes in women's health and holds a doctorate in Nursing Practice (DNP) from Rocky Mountain University of Health Professions, Provo, Utah.

At age 62, Dr. Mimi entered her first bodybuilding competition, making her "Debut at 62," and placed fifth in the Figure Over 40 category. Today, she works with nurse practitioners, healthcare professionals and busy, on-the-go women and men—empowering them with the tools, know-how, and coaching, to transform their health and lives.

Mimi does this in collaboration with her daughter, Kat (Professional Bodybuilder and Health

Coach) and their business *Coach Kat and Dr. Mimi* www.CoachKatandDoctorMimi.com.

Dr. Secor is a guest lecturer at nurse practitioner programs in New England and around the country. She has also published extensively, including her 2014 co-authored textbook, *Advanced Health Assessment of Women; Skills and Procedures,* that was recently selected as a 2016 "AJN Book of the Year-honorable mention," her 2012 co-authored textbook, *Fast Facts About the Gynecologic Exam for Nurse Practitioners: Conducting the GYN Exam in a Nutshell,* and now her NEW book, *Debut a New You: A Guide to Transforming Your Life at Any Age,* already a #1 International Best Seller.

She has years of media experience, including hosting a national NP radio program, *Partners in Practice* on ReachMD. She has also been a guest on *Good Morning America,* interviewed by the *Wall Street Journal, Boston Globe* and many other media publications. Dr. Mimi has received several awards, most notably, the 2013 Lifetime Achievement Award from the Massachusetts Coalition of Nurse Practitioners (MCNP), and the 2015 Student Service Award from Rocky Mountain University for her contributions to the NP profession.

Book Bonuses

"Please get the fantastic bonuses my daughter and I created to help you jumpstart your success. I think you're going to love it!"
-Dr. Mimi

To get the 24 hour Solution go to:
www.DebutANewYou.com